HIDDEN
IN PLAIN
SIGHT

*What We Believe
Really Does Matter*

JOHN MARINELLI

Hidden in Plain Sight
Copyright ©2021 by Rev. John Marinelli
All rights reserved.
First Edition: 2021

Print ISBN: 978-1-0879-1554-8
eBook ISBN: 978-1-0879-1555-5

Contact:
P. O. Box 831413
Ocala, FL. 34483

Cover and Formatting: Streetlight Graphics

No part of this book may be reproduced, scanned, or distributed in any printed or electronic form without permission. Please do not participate in or encourage piracy of copyrighted materials in violation of the author's rights. Thank you for respecting the hard work of this author.

TABLE OF CONTENTS

Preface vii

Introduction ix

Chapter One
    Intelligent Design - Proof That God Exists 1

Chapter Two
    Indisputable Evidence 9

Chapter Three
    Hearing The Voice of God 15

Chapter Four
    Hidden In Plain Sight 25

Chapter Five
    The Incarnation of Christ 37

Chapter Six
    Just, "One Way"
    To God - Believe It or Not 46

Chapter Seven
    First Born Theology 51

Chapter Eight
    Absolute Means Absolute 57

Chapter Nine
    Building A Christian Mindset 75

Chapter Ten
    Hooks To Hang Your Faith On 102

Chapter Eleven
    Finding God's Will For Your Life 116

Chapter Twelve
    Final Authority - Believe It or Not 140

Chapter Thirteen
    Free Will And The Sovereignty
    of God - Believe It or Not 145

Chapter Fourteen
    Heaven Is A Real Place - Believe It or Not 153

Chapter Fifteen
    Hell, A Place of Suffering - Believe It or Not 159

Chapter Sixteen
    The Devil Is Your Enemy - Believe It Not 164

Chapter Seventeen
    The Rapture of
    The Church - Believe It or Not 171

Chapter Eighteen
    Final Judgment - Believe It or Not 177

Chapter Nineteen
    The End of The World - Believe It or Not 183

Chapter Twenty
    Spiritual Warfare - Believe It or Not … 189

Chapter Twenty-One
    Salvation By Grace - Believe It or Not … 196

Chapter Twenty-Two
    The Gifts of The Spirit Are
    For Today - Believe It or Not … 201

Chapter Twenty-Three
    The Body of Christ - Believe It or Not … 209

Chapter Twenty-Four
    Joint Heirs With Christ … 213

Conclusion … 227

About The Author … 229

PREFACE

This is a "Build Your Faith" Biblical teaching that is sure to bring a sense of finality to your Christian lifestyle. It is my hope that you will gain strength in your inner being and courage to walk by faith in this less than perfect world.

I will be using the KJV of the Bible to document all that I say and will on occasion refer to other Bible teachers.

The subject matter was selected because it is in proximity to each other and is themed around Christian beliefs and the study of God. What we believe really does matter.

INTRODUCTION

God has a tendency of hiding truth in plain sight. Sometimes we stumble over it as we walk by faith. However, knowing the truth will bring great faith to any searching soul.

But what truth do we accept? In today's world everyone has his or her own brand of truth. Plus, we struggle under the expectations of others. They are like voices that strive to influence our decisions and change our way of thinking. It could be by way of radio and television, co-workers, family, friends and even doctors. Nevertheless, what we believe really does matter.

Everybody has something to say about what you should or should not be doing with your life. Whose report/opinion are you going to believe?

I see theses voices as special reports delivered to me by supposedly well meaning folks. I even use to listen to them and tried to apply their advice…that was until I became a child of God and read the Bible.

The Bible says in the Old Testament…

Who hath believed our report? and to whom is the arm of the Lord revealed? Isaiah 53

The text refers to a prophecy given by Isaiah thousands of years before the birth of Christ. It was a report that announced the coming of the Messiah as a suffering servant, which was against the thinking of that day.

Isaiah declared the Word of God and posed a question, "whose report will you believe…the voices of the day or the voice of God?

Christianity is under attack in our generation and the voice of God has been ignored. The truth is being presented as a lie and the lie as the truth. This could be no more clear that the lie that says, "There is no God or how about evolution?"

Well I am here to tell you that we didn't come from monkeys and God does exist. But you will have to decide that for yourself. **Whose report will you believe?** Will it be evolution that sits on the premise of natural selection? Or will it be the report found in the Bible that reveals the character and nature of God?

This book is a collection of Biblical teachings that focuses on the existence of God, His handy-work, hearing His voice and being His child.

We will discuss, "Intelligent Design" as proof on God's existence and rebuttal against the lie of evolution. Then we will look at how to hear the voice of God and what He said about a lot of things. We will also discover the words of Jesus as He speaks through the eyewitness accounts of the apostles.

CHAPTER ONE

Intelligent Design
Proof That God Exists

I believe that we can know for sure that God really exists by studying His creation. One of the most striking evidences is, "Intelligent Design." It is hidden in plain sight so as to reveal the existence of God and His handiwork.

Let's ponder the watch. I will use it as an example to show the concept of Intelligent Design.

One account of the origin of the word "watch" is that it came from the Old English word *woecce* which meant "watchman", because it was used by town watchmen to keep track of their shifts. Another says that the term came from 17th century sailors, who used the new mechanisms to time the length of their shipboard *watches* (duty shifts). Wikipedia

The main parts of a simple mechanical watch include: The Mainspring, which provides the power. The Balance Wheel and Hairspring, which oscillate, thereby marking the division of time. By the end of WWII almost all enlisted men wore a wristwatch.

The most complex watch has 1725 parts. The simple wristwatch has little as 51 parts.

What are the odds of all the parts coming together by themselves in one place and at one time to join together in exactly the right positions to make a working watch? I am not a mathematician but I'd estimate the odds to be hundreds of trillions to one that this could never happen. It would be safe to say that it is impossible.

Can Anything Make Itself?

The sum of all the parts does not make the item. Why, because each part has to be fashioned to do a certain job and must be made in such a way as to interact with other parts. Everything that is made must have a maker in order for the item to work. The outcome is never based upon a random act of evolution over an extended period of time.

If we go back to the watch and see 1728 parts on a tree stump, sitting there for billions of years, we will right away realize that they will corrode, rust and become useless. They have no power in themselves to join together.

How then can a single cell evolve into billions of cells with specific functions? You can claim because of DNA but DNA supports an "Intelligent Design" theory that says there is a Divine Maker.

Mixing billions of years with lots of different chemicals can only produce a soup of chemical mush. It has no power to create life.

Michael Behe and Stephen Meyer of the Discovery Institute Explain the Inference to Design.

How do we recognize design? How do we realize that something has been put together intentionally by an intelligent agent? What is intelligent design? Our minds recognize the effects of other intelligent beings when we see the purposeful arrangement of parts, such as the letters and words in a book. Or, the intentional design of something like Mt. Rushmore. We know from our own experience that such things as books and art only come from one source, a creative mind. So, when we see intentionally designed systems and purposeful arrangement of parts, we know that an intelligent agent must be the cause.

The theory of intelligent design simply says that certain features of the universe and of living things are best explained by an intelligent cause, not an undirected process such as natural selection.

The biochemist, Michael Behe helped spark a revolution with his book Darwin's Black Box. Behe inspired a new generation of scientists and thinkers who are now challenging Darwinian evolution and exploring evidence in nature of intelligent design.

Learn about Behe's journey, how those opposed to his ideas tried to kill intelligent design in federal court, and how recent scientific discoveries have vindicated and extended his work.

www:revolutionarybehe.com, features more info about Dr. Behe's research, other molecular machines, evidence for intelligent design, and the stories of revolutionary scientists changing the evolutionary paradigm. They are those that discovered what was hidden in plain sight for generations.

From bacterial propulsion systems to human DNA, evidence of intelligent design is everywhere

By Stephen C. Meyer

What telltale signs of intelligence do we see in living organisms? Over the last 25 years, scientists have discovered an exquisite world of nanotechnology within living cells. Inside these tiny labyrinthine enclosures, scientists have found functioning turbines, miniature pumps, sliding clamps, complex circuits, rotary engines, and machines for copying, reading and editing digital information. It is hardly the simple "globules of plasm" envisioned by Darwin's contemporaries.

Moreover, most of these circuits and machines depend on the co-ordinated function of many separate parts. For example, scientists have discovered that bacterial cells are propelled by miniature rotary engines called flagellar motors that rotate at speeds up to 100,000 rpm.

These engines look as if the Mazda Corporation designed them, with many distinct mechanical parts (made of proteins) including rotors, stators, O-rings, bushings, U-joints, and drive shafts.

Is this appearance of design merely illusory? Could natural selection have produced this appearance in a neo-Darwinian fashion one tiny incremental mutation at a time? Biochemist Michael Behe argues 'no.' He points out that the flagellar motor depends upon the coordinated function of 30 protein parts.

Yet the absence of any one of these parts results in the complete loss of motor function. Remove one of the necessary proteins (as scientists can do experimentally) and the rotary motor simply doesn't work. The motor is, in Behe's terminology, "irreducibly complex."

This creates a problem for the Darwinian mechanism. Natural selection preserves or "selects" functional advantages. If a random mutation helps an organism survive, it can be preserved and passed on to the next generation.

Yet, the flagellar motor has no function until after all of its 30 parts have been assembled. The 29 and 28-part versions of this motor do not work. Thus, the theory of natural selection can "select" or preserve the motor once it has risen, as a functioning whole, but it can do nothing to help build the motor in the first place.

This leaves the origin of molecular machines like the flagellar motor unexplained by natural selection. Darwin specifically taught his theory of saving the best and passing it on to the next generation as a replacement for the design hypothesis.

Is there a better alternative? Based upon our uniform and repeated experience, we know of only one type of cause that produces irreducibly complex systems, namely, intelligence. Indeed, whenever we encounter irreducibly complex systems — such as an integrated circuit or an internal combustion engine — and we know how they arose, invariably a designing engineer played a role.

Thus, Behe concludes — based on our knowledge of what it takes to build functionally integrated complex systems — that intelligent design best explains the origin of molecular machines within cells. Molecular machines appear designed because they were designed.

The strength of Behe's design argument can be judged in part by the response of his critics. After nearly ten years, they have mustered only a vague just-so story about the flagellar motor arising from a simpler subsystem of the motor a tiny syringe-that is sometimes found in bacteria without the other parts of the flagellar motor present. Unfortunately for advocates of this theory, recent genetic studies show that the syringe arose after the flagellar motor-that if anything the syringe evolved from the motor, not the motor from the syringe.

But consider an even more fundamental argument for design. In 1953 when Watson and Crick elucidated the structure of the DNA molecule, they made a startling discovery.

The structure of DNA allows it to store information in the form of a four-character digital code. Strings of precisely sequenced chemicals called nucleotide bases store and transmit the assembly instructions–the information–for building the crucial protein molecules and machines the cell needs to survive.

Francis Crick later developed this idea with his famous "sequence hypothesis" according to which the chemical constituents in DNA function like letters in a written language or symbols in a computer code.

Just as English letters may convey a particular message depending on their arrangement, so too do certain sequences of chemical bases along the spine of a DNA molecule convey precise instructions for building proteins. The arrangement of the chemical characters determines the function of the sequence as a whole.

Thus, the DNA molecule has the same property of "sequence specificity" that characterizes codes and language. As Richard Dawkins has acknowledged, "the machine code of the genes is uncannily computer-like." As Bill Gates has noted, "DNA is like a computer program, but far, far more advanced than any software we've ever created."

After the early 1960s, further discoveries made clear that the digital information in DNA and RNA is only part of a complex information processing system-an advanced form of nanotechnology that both mirrors and exceeds our own in its complexity, design logic and information storage density.

Where did the digital information in the cell come from? And how did the cell's complex information processing system arise? Today these questions lie at the heart of origin-of-life research.

Clearly, the informational features of the cell at least appear designed. And to date no theory of undirected chemical evolution has explained the origin of the digital information needed to build the first living cell. Why? It's because it can't be done.

There is simply too much information in the cell to be explained by chance alone. And the information in DNA has also been shown to defy explanation by reference to the laws of chemistry. It would otherwise be like saying that a newspaper headline might arise as the result of the chemical attraction between ink and paper. Clearly "something else" is at work.

Yet, the scientists arguing for intelligent design do not do so merely because natural processes-chance, laws or the combination of the two-have failed to explain the origin of the information and information processing systems in cells. Instead, they also argue for design because we know from experience that systems possessing these features invariably arise from intelligent causes.

The information on a computer screen can be traced back to a user or programmer. The information in a newspaper ultimately came from a writer-from a mental, rather than a strictly material, cause. As the pioneering information theorist Henry Quastler observed, "information habitually arises from conscious activity."

This connection between information and prior intelligence enables us to detect or infer intelligent activity even from unobservable sources in the distant past. Archeologists infer ancient scribes from hieroglyphic inscriptions.

SETI's search for extraterrestrial intelligence presupposes that information imbedded in electromagnetic signals from space would indicate an intelligent source. As yet, radio astronomers have not found information-bearing signals from distant star systems.

But closer to home, molecular biologists have discovered information in the cell, suggesting — by the same logic that underwrites the SETI program and ordinary scientific reasoning about other informational artifacts — an intelligent source for the information in DNA.

DNA functions like a software program. We know from experience that software comes from programmers. We know generally that information-whether inscribed in hieroglyphics, written in a book or encoded in a radio signal-always arises from an intelligent source.

So the discovery of information in the DNA molecule, provides strong grounds for inferring that intelligence played a role in the origin of DNA, even if we weren't there to observe the system coming into existence.

Thus, contrary to media reports, the theory of intelligent design is not based upon ignorance or religion but instead upon recent scientific discoveries and upon standard methods of scientific reasoning in which our uniform experience of cause and effect guides our inferences about what happened in the past.

Of course, many will still dismiss intelligent design as nothing but warmed over creationism or as a "religious masquerading as science." But intelligent design, unlike creationism, is not based upon the Bible. Design is an inference from biological data, not a deduction from religious authority.

Even so, the theory of intelligent design does provide support for theistic belief. But that is not grounds for dismissing it. To say otherwise confuses the evidence for a theory and its possible implications. Many scientists initially rejected the Big Bang theory because it seemed to challenge the idea of an eternally self-existent universe and pointed to the need for a transcendent cause of matter, space and time.

But scientists eventually accepted the theory despite such apparently unpleasant implications because the evidence strongly supported it. Today a similar metaphysical prejudice confronts the theory of intelligent design.

Nevertheless, it too must be evaluated on the basis of the evidence not our philosophical preferences or concerns about its possible religious implications. Antony Flew, the long-time atheistic philosopher who has come to accept the case for design, insists correctly that we must "follow the evidence wherever it leads."

It should be obvious by now that there was and still is a supernatural mind behind the creation of the universe and life itself. Let me introduce you to Him.

He is The Lord God Jehovah, the true and living God who created everything and watches over it to be sure it all works…and guess what? He does it all just for us. He is the "Watchmaker." It just didn't happen by chance.

CHAPTER TWO

Indisputable Evidence

Here are 10 facts that were hidden in plain sight for years just waiting to be discovered. They support creation as an intelligent design and show evolution as being false.

Moon Dust

Meteoritic dust falls on the earth continually, adding up to thousands, if not millions, of tons of dust per year. Realizing this and knowing that the moon also had meteoritic dust pilling up for what they thought was millions of years, N.A.S.A. scientist were worried that the first lunar ship that landed would sink into many feet of dust which should have accumulated.

However, only about 1/8 of an inch of dust was found, indicating a young moon. The assumption is, that if the 1/8 thickness is evident on the moon, it also has to be the same for the earth because they are in close proximity.

Meteoritic material contributes nickel to the oceans. Taking the amount of nickel in the oceans and the supply from meteoritic dust yields over the years indicates that the age of the earth is only several thousand years, certainly not millions as evolutionists claim. Thus the nickel count in our oceans and meteoritic dust deposits found on the earth clearly indicates a younger planet. These facts tell us that evolution is mot a valid theory.

Magnetic Field

The earth's magnetic field is decaying rapidly at a constant rate. Using this rate of decline, one can back step and determine the magnetism of the earth. 8,000 years ago, the earth would have equaled that of a magnetic star, a highly unlikely occurrence. Also, if electric currents in the earth's core were responsible for the earth's magnetism, the heat generated would have dissolved the earth. This is another fact that shows evolution to be false.

Fossil Record

Charles Darwin stated, in his Origin of Species, "The geological record is extremely imperfect and this fact will, to a large degree, explain why we do not find intermediate varieties, connecting together all the extinct and existing forms of life by the finest graduated steps. He who rejects these views on the nature of the geological record will rightly reject my whole theory."

Now, over 130 years and billions of fossils later, we can rightly reject the view of an incomplete fossil record or of one, "Connecting together all forms of life by the finest graduated steps."

Out of millions of fossils in the world, not one transitional form has been found. All known species show up abruptly in the fossil record, without intermediate forms, thus contributing to the fact of special creation.

Probability

The science of probability has not been favorable to the evolutionary theory. Dr. James Coppedge, of the Center for Probability Research in Biology in California, made some amazing calculations.

Dr. Coppedge applied all the laws of probability studies to the probability of a single cell coming into existence by chance. He computed a world in which the entire crust of the earth…all the oceans; all the atoms and the whole crust were available. He then had these amino acids bind at a rate one and one-half trillion times faster than they do in nature.

In computing the possibilities, he found that to provide a single protein molecule by chance combination would take 10, to the 262nd power, years to get a single cell. (That is, the number 1 followed by 262 zeros)

The single smallest living cell known to mankind – which is called the mycroplasm hominis H39, would take 10, to the 119,841 power, years. That means that if you took thin pieces of paper and wrote 1 and then wrote zeros after it, you would fill up the entire known universe with paper before you could ever even write that number. That is how many years it would take to make one living cell, smaller than any human cell!

According to Emile Borel, a French scientist and expert in the area of probability, an event on the cosmic level with a probability of less than 1 out of 10, to the 50th power, will not happen. The probability of producing one human cell by chance is 10, to the 119,000 power.

Sir Fred Hoyle, British mathematician and astronomer, was quoted in Nature magazine, November 12, 1981, as saying "The chance that higher life forms might have emerged in this way (evolution) is comparable with the chance that a tornado sweeping through a junkyard might assemble a Boeing 747 from the materials therein."

Second Law of Thermodynamics

The second law of thermodynamics states that although the total amount of energy remains constant, the amount of usable energy is constantly decreasing. This law can be seen in most everything. Where work is done, energy is expelled. That energy can never again be used. As usable energy decreases, decay increases. Herein lies the problem for evolution. If the natural trend is toward degeneration, then evolution is impossible, for it demands the betterment of organisms through mutation.

Sun's Diameter

The sun's diameter is shrinking at the rate of five feet per hour. At this rate, life could not have existed on the earth 100,000 years ago because the sun's heat output would have rendered the earth inhabitable.

Earth's Rotation

The spin rate of the earth is slowing by .00002 seconds per year. If the earth were billions of years old, as the evolutionists say it is, the centrifugal force would have notably deformed the earth billions of years ago.

Written Record

The 22nd edition of Robert Young's concordance lists thirty-seven ancient written accounts which all place the date for creation at no earlier than 7000 B.C.

The Bible

Finally, and most importantly, the Bible says that God created the universe and every living thing, so the world must have been created. In denying this, we call God a liar.

Whose Report Will You Believe, Evolution or the Word of God? The facts were hidden in plain sight for all tosee nut some folks just won't look at them.

SOURCES... Baker, Sylvia. Evolution: Bone of Contention (Phillipsburg. N.J.: Evangelical Press. 1986) Second Edition. p.25) Sunderland, Luther D., Darwin's Enigma. Fossils and Other Problems (El Cajon, CA: Master Books 1988). P. 74 Parker, Gary. Life Before Birth (El Cajon, CA: Master Books 1987), pp. 41-44 Chick, Jack T., Primal Man? (Chino, CA. Chick Publications. 1976). P. 23 Cook, Charles, "God's Young Earth signature," Bible-Science Newsletter, August 1989 p. 5

The above evidences against evolution are taken from Kevin Martin's 17 reasons against evolution website.
http://www.jesus-is-savior.com/Evolution%20Hoax/evidences.htm

THE LIGHTHOUSE

A lighthouse is a blessing,
To the ships that toss in the sea,
For it shows them the way,
Until they can clearly see.

The rage of an angry storm
Cannot hide its brilliant light.
Nor can its awesome furry,
Rule as an endless night.

Jesus is the lighthouse,
For those who have gone astray.
The light of His love,
Offers a new and living way.

Jesus is the lighthouse,
When fear and sickness rage.
The light of His love,
Gives hope in difficult days.

So trust in the Lord,
And look for His light.
He alone is "The Lighthouse",
That guides you through the night.

Written by John Marinelli

CHAPTER THREE

Hearing The Voice of God

Whose report will you believe? Will it be the voices that flood your mind and dreams with impure thoughts or will it be what God says?

God is not a mystical floating essence that cannot be touched, seen or otherwise known. He is not somewhere off in a distance, having little or no contact with humanity.

We can know our creator. It is His wish for us to communicate with Him and even have continual fellowship. In fact, He wants to be an intricate part of our lives.

According to the Moody Handbook of Theology, written by Paul P. Enns, Some thirty-eight hundred times the Bible declares, "God said," or "Thus sayeth the Lord"

Here are a few to ponder

And God Said

Genesis 1 & 2

1. Let there be light.

Light dispels darkness and reveals that which exist. Truth and reality all of a sudden becomes clear.

2. Let there be a firmament

(the heavens Or The Sky, Especially When Regarded As A Tangible Thing.) In The Midst Of The Waters, And Let It Divide The Waters From The Waters.

When The Enemy Comes In Like A Flood Of Waters, God Speaks And Divides The Waters From Themselves To Establish A Tangible Reality…No more confusion.

3. Let the waters under the heaven be gathered together unto one place, and let the dry land appear:

God will always allow dry land to appear so we can see our destiny. The land is a picture of our habitation in God.

4. Let the *earth bring forth* grass,

the herb yielding seed, and the fruit tree yielding fruit after his kind, whose seed is in itself, upon the earth:

God never leaves us in a baron place with no provisions. He will always speak to the earth to bring forth exactly what we need.

5. Let there be lights in the firmament of the heaven to divide the day from the night; and let them be for signs, and for seasons, and for days, and years…And let them be for lights in the firmament of the heaven to give light upon the earth:

God makes sure that we have signs to guide us through life. He gives us order and takes away chaos. We are never left alone to figure it out. Our steps are even ordered by the Lord.

6. Let the *waters bring forth* abundantly the moving creature that hath life, and fowl that may fly above the earth in the open firmament of heaven.

God will also speak to the waters commanding them to bring forth life in abundance that we may not be alone.

7. Let the *earth bring forth* the living creature after his kind, cattle, and creeping thing, and beast of the earth after his kind:

The earth will also bring us animals and beast to care for and rule over. We are their caregivers.

8. Let us make man in our image, after our likeness: and let them have dominion over the fish of the sea, and over the fowl of the air, and over the cattle, and over all the earth, and over every creeping thing that creeps upon the earth.

God will raise us up to be rulers over creation…our world, not someone else'. We are in His image to fellowship with Him.

These are the *generations* of the heavens and of the earth when they were created, in the day that the LORD God made the earth and the heavens and every plant of the field before it was in the earth, and every herb of the field before it grew:

Things To Take Note of

1. Only God can create living things.
2. God's creation was done with man in mind.
3. When God speaks, things happen.
4. The beginning always looks ahead to the end to be sure that the destiny is still on course.
5. The central theme of creation, when God Said, was *Fellowship* between God and Man.

"For as the rain cometh down, and the snow from heaven, and returns not, but waters the earth, and makes it bring forth and bud, that it may give seed to the sower, and bread to the eater: So shall my word be that goes forth out

of my mouth: it shall not return unto me void, but it shall accomplish that which I please, and it shall prosper in the thing whereto I sent it." Isaiah 55:10-11

And God Said

Exodus Chapter 20
The Ten Commandments
And God spake all these words, saying,

I am the Lord thy God, which have brought thee out of the land of Egypt, out of the house of bondage.

¹ **Thou shalt have no other gods before me.**

A god is anything that you esteem or worship more than the true and living God. It can be the opposite sex, a material possession, money, power, self, etc.

² **Thou shalt not make unto thee any graven image, or any likeness of any thing that is in heaven above, or that is in the earth beneath, or that is in the water under the earth.** Thou shalt not bow down thyself to them, nor serve them: for I the Lord thy God am a jealous God, visiting the iniquity of the fathers upon the children unto the third and fourth generation of them that hate me; and shewing mercy unto thousands of them that love me, and keep my commandments.

A graven image is a statue or picture of a false deity. It is an image of what you desire to worship.

³ **Thou shalt not take the name of the Lord thy God in vain; for the Lord will not hold him guiltless that takes his name in vain.**

It is a prohibition of blasphemy, specifically, the misuse or "taking in vain" of the name of the God of Israel, or using His name to commit evil.

⁴ *Remember the Sabbath day, to keep it holy.*

Six days shalt thou labor, and do all thy work: But the seventh day is the Sabbath of the Lord thy God: in it thou shalt not do any work, thou, nor thy son, nor thy daughter, thy manservant, nor thy maidservant, nor thy cattle, nor thy stranger that is within thy gates:

For in six days the Lord made heaven and earth, the sea, and all that in them is, and rested the seventh day: wherefore the Lord blessed the Sabbath day, and hallowed it.

The Sabbath is the day that God rested from all His works. We are to rest as well from all our works because we know that in resting, God took into account our needs and provided for them in advance. That's why we keep it holy.

⁵ *Honor thy father and thy mother: that thy days may be long upon the land which the Lord thy God gives thee.*

This is a commandment with a promise. We can be sure that if we honor those who raised us and sacrificed for us that we will live long upon the earth. It's a matter of respect thru love.

⁶ *Thou shalt not kill.*

Killing is wrong, especially if it is a baby in the womb. Killing is not defending ourselves or protecting our families. It is a deliberate taking of life that God brought into existence and blessed.

⁷ *Thou shalt not commit adultery.*

Immorality is viewed through the eyes of adultery, which is treason against that which is holy. It begins in the mind and feeds off sexual thoughts that grow into actions that dishonor. It is a sin against our very soul.

⁸ *Thou shalt not steal.*

Steeling is an act of rebellion against God who is our provider. It is a visual denial of God's will and is rooted in man's lust for power and fame.

⁹ ***Thou shalt not bear false witness against thy neighbor.***

To bear false witness is to tell a lie about someone. The intent is to destroy, discredit, shame or lessen their image among society.

¹⁰ ***Thou shalt not covet thy neighbor's house; thou shalt not covet thy neighbor's wife, or his manservant, or his maidservant, or his ox, or his ass, or anything that is thy neighbor's.***

To covet is to yearn to possess or have (something). God applies this to our neighbor's house, his wife, his material possessions, anything that he owns… we are to be content with what we have and trust that God will bless us as He sees fit to meet the needs of our destiny.

Matthew 4:4

But he answered and said, "It is written, Man shall not live by bread alone, but by every word that proceeds out of the mouth of God."

This is Jesus speaking as recorded in Matthew. His message is very clear. We are to center our lives, our very existence, in what God is saying to us. It is the only way to have life and have it with God's blessing. If we listen to all the other voices and live in their words, we will no doubt go astray from God's perfect will and miss our divine destiny.

Now Hear This >>>>> In order to live by every word that is coming from God, we need to be listening. Hearing God is essential to structuring our lives. The path to peace, happiness, fulfillment and even the afterlife is found in the word of God. We must be listening, searching and always ready to hear. He must be our first priority.

Hebrews 4:12

"For the word of God is quick, and powerful, and sharper than

any two-edged sword, piercing even to the dividing asunder of soul and spirit, and of the joints and marrow, and is a discerner of the thoughts and intents of the heart." Hebrews 4:12

The Word of God is the Bible. It is where we hear from God and are instructed in righteousness. It is our lifeline to eternity. Ignore it and miss His will. Distort it and fall under its judgments. Embrace it and find life, liberty and peace.

II Timothy 3:16

"All scripture is given by inspiration of God, and is profitable for doctrine, for reproof, for correction, for instruction in righteousness:"

The Bible is often referred to as, "Scripture." The apostle Paul tells us in 2nd Timothy that we can trust the Word of God and use it for instruction, correction, reproof and to formulate our doctrine or the way we think and live.

Promises of God

II Corinthians 1:20

"For all the promises of God *in Him are "Yes", and "In Him" Amen, to the glory of God."*

Hidden in the Word of God are great and precious promises that God has spoken to His children. They are hidden in plain sight just waiting for us to discover them and apply them. In fact, there are over 3,000 promises, beginning in Genesis and going all the way to Revelation. God has made promises to us and His words are not empty but full of blessings and love.

These are not flippant, casual promises such as we often make; the promises of God are rock-solid, unequivocal commitments made by God Himself. Because God is faithful, the recipients of the divine promises can have full assurance that what God has pledged will indeed be realized.

And Jesus Said

John, the apostle, tells us in his 1st gospel message that the "Word" was in the beginning. Here's how it reads in the KJV.

> *"In the beginning was the Word, and the Word was with God, and the Word was God." John 1:1*

Note that the Word was with and the Word was.

John goes on to reveal who the Word really is. He says,

> *"The same was in the beginning with God. All things were made by him; and without him was not any thing made that was made. In him was life; and the life was the light of men.*
>
> *And the light shineth in darkness; and the darkness comprehended it not. There was a man sent from God, whose name was John. The same came for a witness, to bear witness of the Light, that all men through him might believe. He was not that Light, but was sent to bear witness of that Light. That was the true Light, which lighteth every man that cometh into the world. He was in the world, and the world was made by him, and the world knew him not.*
>
> *He came unto his own, and his own received him not. But as many as received him, to them gave he power to become the sons of God, even to them that believe on his name: Which were born, not of blood, nor of the will of the flesh, nor of the will of man, but of God. And the Word was made flesh, and dwelt among us, (and we beheld his glory, the glory as of the only begotten of the Father,) full of grace and truth."*

This makes it clear that Jesus was with God in the beginning and was God from the beginning. We can rest easy knowing that what Jesus said is true and reliable. We can trust in Him always. Here are a few things that Jesus said:

1. *I am the way, the truth, and the life: no man comes to the Father, but by me.* –John 14:6

2. *Don't use oaths, whether 'by heaven' or 'by earth' or by anything else. When you say yes or no let it be plain 'Yes' or 'No'.* –Matthew 5:34-37

3. *But seek first the kingdom of God, and His righteousness; and all these things shall be added unto you.* –Matthew 6:33

4. *Ask and it will be given. Seek and you will find. Knock and the door will be opened for you.* –Luke 11:9

5. *If I drive out demons by the finger of God, then the Kingdom of God has arrived for you.* –Mathew 12:2

6. *But I say to you, love your enemies, bless those who curse you, do good to those who hate you, and pray for those who spitefully use you and persecute you,.* –Matthew 5:44

7. *Judge not, and ye shall not be judged: condemn not, and ye shall not be condemned: forgive, and ye shall be forgiven:.* –Luke 6:37

8. *And he that takes not his cross, and follows after me, is not worthy of me.* Matthew 10:38

9. *Then spake Jesus again unto them, saying, I am the light of the world: he that follows me shall not walk in darkness, but shall have the light of life.* John 8:12

10. *And, lo, I am with you always, even unto the end of the world.* Matthew 28:20b

Some Final Thoughts

There are many more commandments, teaching and prophetic sayings in the Bible. It is all the Word of God. All you have to do is read as though God is speaking directly to you. You will receive the wisdom of God, the knowledge of the truth and an abundance of faith to believe.

The important thing to know is that God is always calling your name to come to Him for help, love, fellowship and direction. He will never let you down or disappoint you.

Read His Word and let Him speak to you through the scriptures. Then you too can say, "And God Said" to me. You will hear His voice loud and clear.

CHAPTER FOUR

Hidden In Plain Sight

The Bible is full of Imagery, Word Pictures and Metaphors. God uses them to layer divine truth so as to hide His revelation in plain sight until He is ready to reveal His plan.

Our quest to know in whom we have believed must take into account the diligent study of each context of every scripture passage to be sure that we get the deeper revelation. However, we cannot use the search for spiritual knowledge to create our own private interpretation.

What we see in the scriptures must line up with established truth that has already been acknowledged as divine revelation. Salvation is an excellent example. We know, from multiple Bible sources that Jesus is the only way to God, The Father. He said so Himself...

> *"Jesus saith unto him, I am the way, the truth, and the life: no man cometh unto the Father, but by me."* John 14:6

Paul, the apostle also asserts that Jesus is the only way...

> *"Neither is there salvation in any other: for there is none other name under heaven given among men, whereby we must be saved."* Acts 12:14

If we try to manipulate God's word to say other than what is already clearly revealed, we error and the truth is not in us and we become another anti-Christ.

This chapter will look at Biblical expressions and examine them for divine revelation that may be hidden in plain sight. I am not looking for that which is not already known but am seeking fresh validation of God's will and plan for our lives. It's all there. It just needs to be discovered.

Let's look into the book of beginnings, Genesis and see what the Spirit has to say. I have chosen Genesis 1:1-5. This is the 1st day of creation. It is where God begins. However, to begin requires pre-established thought that formulates concepts and ideas.

We know that God is not haphazard. His actions are in accord with pre-established plans that have been carefully examined and formulated. It is as if God were the master architect that drew up a set of plans for a building that included every little detail.

The plan was established before the work began. That's how God works. He follows a plan that was established long before He takes action. A good example of this is the crucifixion.

> *"Forasmuch as ye know that ye were not redeemed with corruptible things, as silver and gold, from your vain conversation received by tradition from your fathers; But with the precious blood of Christ, as of a lamb without blemish and without spot: Who verily was foreordained before the foundation of the world, but was manifest in these last times for you, Who by him do believe in God, that raised him up from the dead, and gave him glory; that your faith and hope might be in God.* I Peter 1:18-21

> *"And all that dwell upon the earth shall worship him, whose names are not written in the book of life of the Lamb slain from the foundation of the world."* Revelation 13:8

Note that the idea of Jesus being crucified for the sins of the entire world was in the mind of God and became the center of His plan before the world was even formed.

This is how God works. His plan for your life and mine was finished before we ever came on the scene. It's a comforting thought to know that God knew what we would have to face every day and long ago made the provision. Our quest in life is to look for those provisions instead of getting all caught up in worry, stress and depression. We are challenged, by the Word of God, to "Fear Not." But only to Believe.

The 1st Day of The Rest of Our Lives

"In the beginning God created the heaven and the earth. And the earth was without form, and void; and darkness was upon the face of the deep. And the Spirit of God moved upon the face of the waters. And God said, Let there be light: and there was light. And God saw the light, that it was good: and God divided the light from the darkness. And God called the light Day, and the darkness he called Night. And the evening and the morning were the first day."
Genesis 1:1-5

Consider the 1st day of creation as if it were the 1st day of our new life in Christ. It all starts with God and it begins, *"In the beginning."*

Everything has a beginning but not everything begins with God. He has given man a free fill to create his own destiny that begins with the choice of Godly counsel or unholy alliances. We make such a choice every day as we get up every morning and go about our day.

However, if we are a "God Seeker," we will desire Godly counsel and request it in prayer as we commune with the Lord. This puts God in our beginnings and quite frankly, it will take the power and wisdom of God to get through these trying times. It is comforting to know that our creator is in our beginnings to fashion our days. Read what the Bible says…

> *"This is the day which the Lord hath made; we will rejoice and be glad in it."* Psalm 118:24

We have every reason to rejoice in our day because God has made the day with us in mind. Other folks, that do not believe or seek God's counsel, face an onslaught of trials and suffering or at best a happenstance of mixed encounters.

On the other hand, the Spirit of the living God, whose mission is to manifest the image and likeness of God upon the earth and to see that we make it through life and arrive safely to our destiny, will comfort us continually.

Imagine a day were God's power is actively engaged to protect you from harm: where God's love is bringing multiple blessings to your doorstep: where God's counsel is leading you in every decision: where the day, itself, beckons to your call. This is the day that the Lord has made.

I know what you are thinking. This is just not my reality. However, consider this,

> *"But Jesus beheld them, and said unto them, with men this is impossible; but with God all things are possible."* Matthew 19:26

This is a hidden truth that is in plain sight. The possible can become the reality. All we need to do is believe in God, that He will bring it to pass.

Without Form & Void

"And the earth was without form, and void; and darkness was upon the face of the deep." Genesis 1:2

Have you ever felt that your life had no meaning, that it was void and without form? I have, many times. The devil loves to paint a picture of emptiness, doom and gloom so we fall into despair. He tries to deceive the child of God through illusions and lies about who you are, how you think and what you feel. He wants you to condemn yourself so he can rob you of your life and substance.

Jesus said, *"The thief cometh not, but for to steal, and to kill, and to destroy: I am come that they might have life, and that they might have it more abundantly."* John 10:10

There is another hidden truth here. If your life is *without form and void,* it could be because that void is supposed to be filled with the Holy Spirit and you have not allowed that to happen. In order to have abundant life, as Jesus said, you must first make Jesus your Lord and Savior. His life fills your emptiness and rules over your day to make it rich and meaningful.

And Darkness Was Upon The Face of The Deep

The Bible says a lot about light and darkness. They are often compared with one another to represent the relationship between good and evil. God's children are referred to as children of light... whereas; the ungodly are portrayed as children of darkness.

If we look at the darkness as sin and the deep as the essence of humanity, it reflects the horror of sin and the fall of man from light into darkness that occurred when Adam sinned and lost God's indwelling presence. That is when the void occurred in humanity.

Look at it as a continuation from verse #1 and the without form and void was covered in a cloud of darkness that prevented the light to shine. This is actually a hidden truth concerning "***Total Depravity***." Which is to say, lost and dead in our sins. The dictionary defines Depravity like this:

> The quality or state of being corrupt, evil, or perverted: the quality or state of being depraved.

Some Synonyms are:

> abjection, corruption, corruptness,
> debasement, debauchery, decadence,
> decadency, degeneracy, degenerateness,
> degeneration, degradation,
> demoralization, dissipatedness, dissipation,
> dissoluteness, libertinage,
> libertinism, perversion, pervertedness,
> rakishness, and turpitude.

Moral Corruption; Wicked

Needless to say, when darkness is upon the face of the deep, there is no light, no hope and no escape. This is "***Total Depravity***"

We cannot climb out of the void and the darkness brings with it fear and torment as we grope in the dark, not understanding why we were born, why we are here and what is going to happen next. We are indeed without hope, lost and dead in our sins. Does that sound familiar? Here's what the scriptures say:

> *"And you, being dead in your sins and the uncircumcision of your flesh, hath he quickened together with him, having forgiven you all trespasses;"* Colossians 2:13

> *"And you has he made alive, who were dead in trespasses and sins."* Ephesians 2:1

This is the result of sin. We are left without form and void with darkness covering us so thick that we cannot see the light. This is "Total Depravity" It is a cesspool of wickedness and debauchery.

Only God Can Change Things

"And the Spirit of God moved upon the face of the waters. And God said, let there be light: and there was light. And God saw the light, that it was good: and God divided the light from the darkness." Genesis 1:2b-4

Man cannot save himself. He tries but salvation is beyond his reach. Man continually misses the mark because he is drowning in immorality. It is a part of his nature. God dwells in a state of moral Holiness. Man does not and cannot.

The Face of The Waters That Overwhelms Man

So what can be done to help man reach God's morally righteousness level? It will take a move of the Spirit of God. He must move upon the face of the waters that overwhelm mankind. He must separate the waters, setting boundaries so dry land will appear. This gives man a place to stand, even if he is still in the darkness. It is the 1st step towards his redemption.

The problem with the unsaved is they are in a raging sea with no sight of dry land. They are caught in the currents of sin and swept away into evil plots and demonic traps. All of this was hidden in darkness until the Spirit of God moved upon the waters that overwhelmed man.

God's Word illuminates the path of our lives. If we keep God's Word shining along the way, then we will be far less likely to trip. We will not be easily deceived. Because we are following the light, we will see what the light reveals in the path ahead of us. (Richard T. Ritenbaugh)

Light Equals Truth

God must speak into the darkness of sin and command the light of His truth to shine. Without His intervention, there would be no revelation of truth and man would still be lost and dead in his sin.

> *"O send out thy light and thy truth: let them lead me; let them bring me unto thy holy hill, and to thy tabernacles."*
> Psalm 43:3

In this context, light and truth are basically synonymous. The Hebrews had a way of "doubling-up" or "doubling-over" a word, a term, a phrase; so that one would emphasize the other, despite both meaning essentially the same thing.

This method hits a concept from two slightly different angles so that it becomes more emphatic. Light and truth are the similar ideas, the word "truth" channeling the author's illustration of light and what it signifies. Light illustrates, emphasizes, and expands the abstract idea of truth.

(John W. Ritenbaugh…From Forerunner Commentary)

Separation & Freedom

After God saw that the light He called forth was good, He separated it from the darkness. He does that with man as well. Here's what the Word of God says to us:

> *"Wherefore come out from among them, and be ye separate, saith the Lord, and touch not the unclean thing; and I will receive you."* II Corinthians 6:17

It is obvious that God has separated the darkness from the light in our lives. We cannot now say, "I didn't know any better". We do know good from evil and what is clean and unclean. Freedom is to walk in the light and have no fellowship with the things of darkness.

Day & Night

The day is where the light rules. It brings us truth and revelation from God. The night is the prison where darkness is bound. If you have ever noticed day and night, you will immediately realize that light can and does penetrate darkness but darkness cannot illuminate anything. The light even rules in the midst of darkness, even if it is just a flicker.

When God banished the evil angels from heaven, He placed them in everlasting chains under darkness. Here's how it is expressed in the scriptures:

> *"And the angels which kept not their first estate, but left their own habitation, he hath reserved in everlasting chains under darkness unto the judgment of the great day."* Jude Verse 6

Light & Darkness

> *"Jesus answered, are there not twelve hours in the day? If any man walk in the day, he stumbleth not, because he seeth the light of this world. But if a man walk in the night, he stumbleth, because there is no light in him."* John 11:9-10

The hidden truth is… when you walk in SIN (Darkness), you stumble because there is no Light (Truth) to hold on to. Either we walk in the light or we don't. It is a free will choice. However, those that walk in darkness lose their way because they lay aside the truth.

And God...

"And God called the light Day, and the darkness he called Night. And the evening and the morning were the first day."
Genesis 1:5

I find it interesting that creation was totally in the hands of God. He was in charge and ruled the event first hand.

When we let Him call forth our creation, He becomes our Lord and Savior. Our free will is engaged to seat Him as Lord of Lords. Our destiny is in His hands. He can create it any way He sees fit. His will is what we want and this is how we get it.

When we say, *"And God"* we build an everlasting testimony that stands as a witness to all around us proclaiming Jesus as our Lord. How many events can you attribute to the intervention of God? Here are a few that I can recall:

1. And God... saved my marriage.
2. And God... delivered me from evil spirits.
3. And God... helped me with my finances.
4. And God... blessed me with peace of mind.

I can go on and on. I know I didn't give details on the above events but you should get the point. He (God) did a lot of stuff in my life over the past 76 years, so much so, that I have a history that I can refer to when I get down or confused or even fearful about life. I can go to my library of events that occurred in my relationship with God and find comfort and even draw faith to stand in my hour of need.

You may wish to read one of my other books. The title is, *"Times Past But Not Forgotten"*. It is a stroll down memory lane remembering some major events where God intervened in my life. (ISBN # 978-1-0879-5056-3)

I have two sayings. They go like this... "If He did it then, He'll do it again." "If He didn't do it then, He'll do it now."

We have looked at the 1st day of God's creation to examine it for hidden truths that relate and/or apply to our lives. Here's what we saw:

1. Man, by nature, is depraved or habitually wicked and full of sin.
2. God has the power and desire to redeem man, taking him to a higher plain for divine fellowship.
3. Darkness overshadows man's dwelling place and keeps him from being enlighten.
4. Sin creates a void in the soul of man that has no form or purpose except to lay in waste. It must be filled with the Spirit of God.
5. It will take an act of God to cause man to seek Him for he is blinded by the darkness of his own soul.
6. Light is equal to truth and it must shine into man's soul to bring regeneration.
7. Man, like day and night, must be kept separate from evil in order to function.
8. Man must walk in the light to grow and commune with God.
9. Man's destiny is a God thing. He initiated it and controls it and will finish it.
10. Man can count on God to deliver him and keep him in His grace because God is actively engaged in man's destiny. He is not passive.

THE CREATION GROANS

The creatures' expectations
shall all come true.
Their earnest desire
is to see what God will do.

With groaning and longing,
from deep within,
the creatures wait,
for the deliverance of men.

Subjected to vanity
by the powers to be,
they too shall be delivered,
through the cross of Calvary.

With loving expectations,
all of creation groans inside,
waiting for the sons of God
so they can dwell by their side.

Written By
John Marinelli

CHAPTER FIVE

The Incarnation of Christ

I have chosen to use much of the text being offered by Got/Questions.org to start off this teaching. They do an excellent job of explaining, far better than my attempt. However, I will interject here and there with my own comments.

Incarnation is a term used by theologians to indicate that Jesus, the Son of God, took on human flesh. This is similar to the "Hypostatic Union". The difference is that the hypostatic union explains how Jesus' two natures are joined, and the Incarnation more specifically affirms His humanity.

The word *incarnation* means "the act of being made flesh." It comes from the Latin version of **John 1:14**, which in English reads,

> *"The Word became flesh and made His dwelling among us."*

Because of the near-exclusive use of the Latin Vulgate in the church through the Middle Ages, the Latin term became standard.

Biblical support for Jesus' humanity is extensive. The Gospels report Jesus' human needs including sleep (Luke 8:23), food (Matthew 4:2; 21:18), and physical protection (Matthew 2:13-15; John 10:39).

Other indications of His humanity are that He perspired (Luke 22:43-44) and bled (John 19:34). Jesus also expressed emotions including joy (John 15:11), sorrow (Matthew 26:37), and anger (Mark 3:5). During His life, Jesus referred to Himself as a man (John 8:40), and after His resurrection His humanity was still recognized (Acts 2:22).

Can you believe this report…that God came down from heaven to become a man? Why would He do that?

The Purpose of The Incarnation

But the purpose of the Incarnation was not to taste food or to feel sorrow. The Son of God came in the flesh in order to be the Savior of mankind.

First, it was necessary to be born "under the law" (Galatians 4:4). All of us have failed to fulfill God's Law. Christ came in the flesh, under the Law, to fulfill the Law on our behalf (Matthew 5:17; Galatians 4:5).

Second, it was necessary for the Savior to shed His blood for the forgiveness of sins (Hebrews 9:22). A blood sacrifice, of course, requires a body of flesh and blood and this was God's plan for the Incarnation:

"When Christ came into the world, he said: 'Sacrifice and offering (under the Old Covenant) you did not desire, but a body you prepared for me'" (Hebrews 10:5). Without the Incarnation, Christ could not really die, and the cross is meaningless.

God did an incredible work in sending His only begotten Son into the world and providing us with a salvation we do not deserve. Praise the Lord for that moment in which the, "Word," became flesh. We are now redeemed with the precious blood of Christ, a lamb without blemish or defect (1Peter1:19).

The Hypostatic Union

The hypostatic union is the term used to describe how God the Son, Jesus Christ, took on a human nature, yet remained fully God at the same time. Jesus always had been God (John 8:58, 10:30), but at the incarnation, Jesus became a human being (John 1:14). The addition of the human nature to the divine nature equals Jesus, the God-man. This is the hypostatic union, Jesus Christ, one Person, fully God and fully man.

Jesus' two natures, human and divine, are inseparable. Jesus will forever be the God-man, fully God and fully human, two distinct natures in one person.

Jesus' humanity and divinity are not mixed, but are united without loss of separate identity. Jesus sometimes operated with the limitations of humanity (John 4:6, 19:28) and other times in the power of His deity (John 11:43; Matthew 14:18-21). In both, Jesus' actions were from His one Person. Jesus had two natures, but only one personality.

The doctrine of the hypostatic union is an attempt to explain how Jesus could be both God and man at the same time. It is impossible for us to fully understand how God works. We, as human beings with finite minds, should not expect to totally comprehend an infinite God.

Jesus is both God and man. Jesus has always been God, but He did not become a human being until He was conceived in Mary. Jesus became a human being in order to identify with us in our struggles (Hebrews 2:17) and, more importantly, so that He could die on the cross to pay the penalty for our sins (Philippians 2:5-11).

So, the hypostatic union teaches that Jesus is both fully human and fully divine, that there is no mixture or dilution of either nature, and that He is one united person, forever.

The Importance of God In The Flesh

Since Jesus' conception by the Holy Spirit in the womb of the virgin, Mary (Luke 1:26-38), the real identity of Jesus Christ has always been questioned by skeptics. It began with Mary's fiancé, Joseph, who was afraid to marry her when she revealed that she was pregnant (Matthew 1:18-24). He took her as his wife only after the angel confirmed to him that the child she carried was the Son of God.

Hundreds of years before the birth of Christ, the prophet Isaiah foretold the coming of God's Son:

> *"For to us a child is born, to us a son is given, and the government will be on his shoulders. And he will be called Wonderful Counselor, Mighty God, Everlasting Father, Prince of Peace"* (Isaiah 9:6).

When the angel spoke to Joseph and announced the impending birth of Jesus, he alluded to Isaiah's prophecy:

> *"The virgin will conceive and give birth to a son, and they will call him Immanuel (which means 'God with us')"* (Matthew 1:23).

This did not mean they were to name the baby Immanuel; it meant that "God with us" was the baby's identity. Jesus was God coming in the flesh to dwell with man.

Jesus Himself understood the speculation about His identity. He asked His disciples, *"Who do people say that I am?"* (Matthew 16:13; Mark 8:27). The answers varied, as they do today. Then Jesus asked a more pressing question: *"Who do you say that I am?"* (Matthew 16:15).

Peter gave the right answer: "You are the Christ, the Son of the living God" (Matthew 16:16). Jesus affirmed the truth of Peter's answer and promised that, upon that truth, He would build His church. (Matthew 16:18)

Nature & Identity

The true nature and identity of Jesus Christ has eternal significance. Every person must answer the question Jesus asked His disciples: "Who do you say that I am?"

He gave us the correct answer in many ways. In John 14:9-10, Jesus said,

> *"Anyone who has seen me has seen the Father. How can you say, 'Show us the Father'? Don't you believe that I am in the Father, and that the Father is in me? The words I say to you I do not speak on my own authority. Rather, it is the Father, living in me, who is doing his work."*

The Bible is clear about the divine nature of the Lord Jesus Christ (see John 1:1-14). Philippians 2:6-7 says that, although Jesus was "in very nature God, He did not consider equality with God something to be used to his own advantage; rather, he made himself nothing by taking the very nature of a servant, being made in human likeness." Colossians 2:9 says,

> *"In Christ all the fullness of the Deity lives in bodily form."*

Jesus is fully God and fully man, and the fact of His **incarnation** is of utmost importance. He lived a human life but did not possess a sin nature as we do.

He was tempted but never sinned (Hebrews 2:14-18; 4:15). Sin entered the world through Adam, and Adam's sinful nature has been transferred to every baby born into the world (Romans 5:12)—except for Jesus. Because Jesus did not have a human father, He did not inherit a sin nature. He possessed the divine nature from His Heavenly Father.

(This could have only happened through a "Virgin Birth')

Jesus had to meet all the requirements of a holy God before He could be an acceptable sacrifice for our sin (John 8:29; Hebrews 9:14). He had to fulfill over three hundred prophecies about the Messiah that God, through the prophets, had foretold (Matthew 4:13-14; Luke 22:37; Isaiah 53; Micah 5:2).

Since the fall of man (Genesis 3:21-23), the only way to be made right with God has been the blood of an innocent sacrifice (Leviticus 9:2; Numbers 28:19; Deuteronomy 15:21; Hebrews 9:22).

The Final Sacrifice

Jesus was the final, perfect sacrifice that satisfied forever God's wrath against sin (Hebrews 10:14). His divine nature made Him fit for the work of Redeemer; His human body allowed Him to shed the blood necessary to redeem. No human being with a sin nature could pay such a debt. No one else could meet the requirements to become the sacrifice for the sins of the whole world (Matthew 26:28; 1 John 2:2). If Jesus were merely a good man as some claim, then He had a sin nature and was not perfect. In that case, His death and resurrection would have no power to save anyone.

Because Jesus was God in the flesh, He alone could pay the debt we owed to God. His victory over death and the grave won the victory for everyone who puts their trust in Him (John 1:12; 1 Corinthians 15:3-4, 17).

Both God & Man At The Same Time

The Bible teaches that Jesus Christ is both God and man. Many Christians are understandably confused when it comes to understanding how Jesus can be God and man at the same time. How could our divine Creator become a human? Could a first-century Jewish man really be God?

While a certain amount of mystery will always accompany this issue, both Scripture and, to a lesser extent, church tradition provides for us important distinctions to help us make sense of this matter.

While previous church councils had deliberated over issues pertaining to the nature of Christ and His relationship to the Father, it was the Council of Chalcedon (AD 481) that affirmed that Christ is "the same perfect in divinity and perfect in humanity, the same truly God and truly man."

This statement is not true simply because the council taught it. Rather, the council's declaration was authoritative only insofar as it aligned with what the Bible teaches on the subject.

Scripture is clear that Jesus is God (John 20:28; Titus 2:13; Hebrews 1:8), and it is equally clear that He is truly human (Romans 1:2–4; 1 John 4:2–3). Jesus claimed the divine name (John 8:58) and did things that only God can do (Mark 2:1–12; Luke 7:48–50).

But Jesus also displayed the weaknesses and vulnerabilities common to humanity (Luke 19:41; John 19:28).

The belief that Jesus is both God and man is of fundamental importance. The apostle Paul wrote that an affirmation of the divinity of Jesus is required to be saved (Romans 10:9), and the apostle John provided a sober warning that those who deny Christ's true humanity are promoting the doctrine of antichrist (2 John 1:7).

The Triune God of the Bible has existed and reigned from all eternity, and the second person of the Trinity, the Son, took on human flesh at a particular point in time (Luke 1:35; Hebrews1: 5). God, the Son, added a sinless human nature to His eternally existent divine nature.

The result was the Incarnation. God the Son became a man (John 1:1, 14). Hebrews 2:17 gives the reason that Jesus had to be both God and man: "He had to be made like them, fully human in every way, in order that He might become a merciful and faithful high priest in service to God, and that He might make atonement for the sins of the people." The Son of God took on human flesh to provide redemption to those under the law (Galatians 4:4–5).

At no time did Jesus ever cease to be God. Although He was made fully human, there was never a point when He abrogated His divine nature (see Luke 6:5, 8). It is equally true that, after becoming incarnate, the Son has never ceased to be human. As the apostle Paul wrote,

> *"For there is one God, and there is one mediator between God and men, the man, Christ Jesus"* (1 Timothy 2:5).

Jesus is not half-human and half-divine. Rather, He is *Theanthropos*, the God-man. The Lord Jesus Christ is one eternally divine person who will forever possess two distinct yet inseparable natures: one divine and one human.

The world does not believe this report. There are many so-called Christians that also do not believe this report. However, it is clearly taught in the scriptures.

Whose report will you believe, the Biblical account or those voices around you?

CHAPTER SIX

Just, "One Way" To God Believe It or Not

Chapter Five dealt with the Incarnation of Christ where God became man, fully God and fully man. As mentioned, the purpose was to be the high priest or mediator between God and man. Jesus would forever be the only way to heaven. His name and faith in Him opened the door.

It is hard for most folks that are not "Born Again" to understand why Jesus the only way to God, yet it is true. There is only one way and that is through Jesus Christ.

The Bible is our source to prove that the one-way doctrine is valid. It says,

> *"Neither is there salvation in any other: for there is none other name under heaven given among men, whereby we must be saved."* Acts 4:12

Jesus is the only way to attain salvation. All the world religions cannot save us. Joining a church or specific faith cannot save us.

It must be an acknowledgment of our sin, our cry before the throne of God for forgiveness, and our invitation for Jesus to come into our hearts and save us. His name is the only one that can get us through death into eternal life.

Here are a few scriptures that support the only "One-Way" doctrine.

> *"There is one God, and one mediator between God and men, the man Christ Jesus; Who gave himself a ransom for all, to be testified in due time."* (I Timothy 2:5-6)

> *"Believe on the Lord Jesus Christ and thou shalt be saved"* (Acts 16:31)

> *"That if thou shalt confess with thy mouth the Lord Jesus, and shalt believe in thine heart that God hath raised him from the dead, thou shalt be saved, For with the heart man believeth unto righteousness; and with the mouth confession is made unto salvation."* (Romans 10:9-10)

The skeptic would say, "You mean to tell me that all the religions of the world are wrong and only Christianity is the one true religion?"

Remember, Christianity is not a religion. It is a relationship born out of love between man and the one true and living God. There is no one true religion.

Religion, in itself, will not get us to God. It is the blood of Christ that unlocks the door and our confession of faith in Jesus that makes it all happen. (John 14:6)

Why is Jesus the only way to God?...Because God planned it that way. He set the penalty for sin, which was death.

> *The soul that sinneth, it shall die.* (Ezekiel 18:20)

In fact, Jesus was the slain Lamb of God before the foundation of the world. (Ephesians 1:3-7)

Jesus Himself said, as recorded in the gospel of John.

> *"I am the way, the truth, and the life: No man cometh to the Father but by Me"*. John 14:6

Christianity states that the God of the Bible is the only true God and salvation is only possible by accepting Jesus Christ, His only begotten Son as Savior and Lord.

> *"For he hath made him to be sin for us, who knew no sin; that we might be made the righteousness of God in him."* II Corinthians 5:21

God validated His Son as the only way in multiple ways so we could be assured that Jesus was indeed the only way to Him. Here are some to consider.

1. **He Said So And Proved It With Miracles**…He claimed to be the only way as in John's record 14:6 says but validation came through miracles that proved He was who He claimed to be.

2. **Eyewitnesses…saw Jesus' miracles and validated them as authentic.** Over 500 followers saw Jesus, after His resurrection, and watched Him ascend into heaven.

3. **The Prophets foretold of His coming**, where He would be born, that He would be God in human flesh and lots more…all prophetic statements were realized in Jesus, even those like in Isaiah chapter 53 that were uttered hundreds of years before Jesus came.

4. **God Himself validated Jesus as His sole pathway to Him.** *"While he was still speaking, behold, a bright cloud overshadowed them; and suddenly a voice came out of the cloud, saying, "This is My beloved Son, in whom I am well pleased. Hear ye Him!"* (Mathew 17:5)

5. **The Apostles lost their homes, wealth, and even their lives preaching the gospel.** Would they do that if it were a lie? I don't think so. They testified to the truth and were

willing to die for it if necessary. (See Foxes Book of Martyrs)

6. **Thousands of Believers over several centuries have testified of how Jesus helped them and blessed them.**

7. **My Personal Testimony**…I can personally testify that I have seen the hand of the Lord in my life and communicate with Him daily. I know He is the Christ.

The provability that one man could fulfill all prophecies about a Messiah that God Himself said would come, (Gen.3:15), and perform fantastic miracles while here on earth, and be raised from the dead, and ascend into heaven while hundreds looked on is astronomical.

But Jesus did just that…fulfilled everything that was foretold about the coming Messiah. He had to be who He said He was and therefore is truly the only way to God.

With

WITH EARTHEN VESSELS

Earthen vessels have never shown
such glory that once was known.
Through time and all of eternity,
came the glory of His majesty.

Full of love and full of grace,
He dwelt among the human race
to heal the sick, the blind and the lame,
to free mankind from sin and shame.

With earthen vessel He conquered all
by perfect obedience to His destined call.
For this we praise His holy Name,
full of grace and full of fame.

The glory of His majesty
still shines through from eternity.
Again and again to meet life's call,
in earthen vessels to conquer all.

Written By
John Marinelli

CHAPTER SEVEN

First Born Theology

We are still talking about Jesus. The Bible tells us that in Adam, all die but in Christ, All will be made alive. (Romans Chapter five). Jesus is looked at, in theological circles, as the first born among many brethren.

> *"For whom he did foreknow, he also did predestinate to be conformed to the image of his Son, that he might be the firstborn among many brethren.: Romans 8:29*

Here's what Biblestudyguide.org has to say about that.

Under the Law of Moses, the term "firstborn" was used literally and figuratively, expressing a relationship, an inheritance, preeminence, and privileges.

The firstborn son's inheritance was a double portion. He had special privileges as the firstborn male of the family.

> *"But he shall acknowledge the firstborn, the son of the unloved, by giving him a double portion of all that he has, for he is the beginning of his strength; to him belongs the right of the firstborn"* (Deut. 21:17).

God called Israel His firstborn son. This confirms the relationship

He had with Israel, and the preeminence, privileges, and inheritance He granted the nation.

> *"Then you shall say to Pharaoh, 'Thus says the LORD, Israel is My son, My firstborn"* (Ex. 4:22).

God calls David, who was a type of Christ, His firstborn. This communicates the relationship of David with God, looking forward to the relationship Jesus would have with God.

> *"I also shall make him My firstborn, the highest of the kings of the earth"* (Ps. 89:27).

In Scripture, God uses the term ***"firstborn"*** to communicate several things about Jesus and Christians, which we will investigate here.

Jesus: Firstborn, Preeminent

Jesus is the firstborn of all creation. "He is the image of the invisible God, he firstborn of all creation" (Col. 1:15). The phrase "firstborn over creation" does not mean that God created Jesus, because He's divine and therefore eternal (John 1:1). Rather, it means that He's preeminent.

> *"For by Him all things were created, both in the heavens and on earth, visible and invisible, whether thrones or dominions or rulers or authorities – all things have been created through Him and for Him. He is before all things, and in Him all things hold together. He is also head of the body, the church; and He is the beginning, the firstborn from the dead, so that He Himself will come to have first place in everything"* **(Col. 1:16-18).**

> *"And He put all things in subjection under His feet, and gave Him as head over all things to the church"* (Eph. 1:22).

Jesus: Firstborn From The Dead

Jesus is firstborn from the dead. In other words, He was first to resurrect from the grave, having conquered death.

> *"He is also head of the body, the church; and He is the beginning, the firstborn from the dead, so that He Himself will come to have first place in everything"* (Col. 1:18).

> *"And from Jesus Christ, the faithful witness, the firstborn of the dead, and the ruler of the kings of the earth. To Him who loves us and **released us** from our sins by His blood—"* (Rev. 1:5).

Because Jesus conquered death, and rose by the power granted Him by God (Jn. 10:18), we too will resurrect to eternal life by the power of God if we obey Jesus (1 Cor. 6:14; Heb. 5:9).

Jesus: Firstborn Among Many Brethren

Paul says that Jesus was the firstborn among many brethren.

"For those whom He foreknew, He also predestined to become conformed to the image of His Son, so that He would be the firstborn among many brethren" (Rom. 8:29). Since we are flesh, Jesus became flesh to author our salvation, and save us.

> *"But we do see Him who was made for a little while lower than the angels, namely, Jesus, because of the suffering of death crowned with glory and honor, so that by the grace of God He might taste death for everyone. For it was fitting for Him, for whom are all things, and through whom are all things, in bringing many sons to glory, to perfect the author of their salvation through sufferings. For both He who sanctifies and those who are sanctified are all from one*

Father; for which reason He is not ashamed to call them brethren" (Heb. 2:9-11).

Therefore, since the children share in flesh and blood, He Himself likewise also partook of the same, that through death He might render powerless him who had the power of death, that is, the devil, and might free those who through fear of death were subject to slavery all their lives" (Heb. 2:14-15).

As Christians, we follow in the footsteps of Jesus (1 Pet. 2:24). Therefore, we are His brethren because we have conformed to His image, making Satan powerless against us in respect to death (Heb. 2:9-15).

This means that every "Born Again" believer also has two natures. From God's viewpoint, our body has been redeemed by the sacrifice of Jesus. He became sin for us that we might be the righteousness of God in Him. (Jesus).

"For he has made him, who knew no sin, to be sin for us; that we might be made the righteousness of God in him." II Corinthians 5:21

Then He filled us with His very own Spirit. Like Adam, He breathed into our nostrils the breath of live (His Holy Spirit) and we became alive spiritually. Thus we now are His brethren, Man & God in the same place at the same time.

We can never be gods. Some folks have espoused such a notion but that is not so. We are fully mankind being filled with God's Spirit. We are the image and likeness of God through Jesus. We can never attain a god status.

Church of the Firstborn

Since Jesus is the firstborn, His church is called "church of the firstborn" in Scripture. "To the general assembly and church of the firstborn who are enrolled in heaven, and to God, the Judge of all, and to the spirits of the righteous made perfect" (Heb. 12:23).

Members of the church of the firstborn have a relationship with God, an inheritance from God, preeminence in the world as God's people, and privileges given to them by God. They're enrolled in heaven, and possess eternal life.

But if you're not a Christian, If you're a Christian, you're a member of Jesus' church, the firstborn's church, and have all these blessings you're missing out on the most precious things in life.

The literal meaning of, "Incarnation" is Jesus, the Son of God, taking on human flesh." He did this through the virgin birth. The result of that event was multi-purpose:

1. To redeem mankind.
2. To destroy the works of the devil.
3. To bring many sons into glory as His brethren.
4. To seek out and save that which was lost, which was His image and likeness on the earth.
5. To become the mediator between God and man.
6. To bring the kingdom of God here on earth.
7. To reestablish fellowship between God and man.

I am sure you will come across more benefits to add to this list. This is enough to strengthen our faith and become the basis for our praise and adoration.

Let us always give praise to God, who came from Heaven to become the God-Man for us. He didn't have to do it, yet He did. He is God. We are not. He is not God and Man mingled together. He is fully God dwelling in a fully human body. The only difference between His body and ours in His has no sin.

Do not think that you will ever become a god to rule over nature or any other realm. God is God over everything. If we rule over anything, it will be at His direction and with His guidance. We are joint heirs with Christ, poised to inherit the kingdom. This is our destiny.

CHAPTER EIGHT

Absolute Means Absolute

The Bible has a way of hiding truth in plain sight. Take for example, "Absolute truth." By way of definition, "Absolute Truth" is defined as inflexible reality: fixed, invariable, unalterable facts.

Here is something that is absolute. It is a fixed, invariable, unalterable fact that there are absolutely no square circles and there are absolutely no round squares.

You can't logically argue against the existence of absolute truth. To argue against something is to establish that a truth exists. You cannot argue against absolute truth unless an absolute truth is the basis of your argument. Consider a few of the classic arguments and declarations made by those who seek to argue against the existence of absolute truth.

"There are no absolutes." First of all, the relativist is declaring there are absolutely no absolutes. That is an absolute statement. The statement is logically contradictory. If the statement is true, there is, in fact, an absolute – there are absolutely no absolutes.

"Truth Is Relative." Again, this is an absolute statement implying truth is absolutely relative. Besides positing an absolute, suppose the statement was true and "truth is relative." Everything including that statement would be relative. If a statement is relative, it is not always true.

If "truth is relative" it is not always true. Sometimes truth is not relative. This means there are absolutes, which means the above statement is false. When you follow the logic, relativist arguments will always contradict themselves.

"Who Knows What The Truth Is, Right?" In the same sentence the speaker declares that no one knows what the truth is, then he turns around and asks those who are listening to affirm the truth of his statement.

"No One Knows What The Truth Is." The speaker obviously believes his statement is true.

There are philosophers who actually spend countless hours toiling over thick volumes written on the "meaninglessness" of everything. We can assume they think the text is meaningful!

Then there are those philosophy teachers, who teach their students,

1. "No one's opinion is superior to anyone else's.

2. There is no hierarchy of truth or values.

3. Anyone's viewpoint is just as valid as anyone else's viewpoint.

4. We all have our own truth."

Then they turn around and grade the papers!

Absolute Truth And Morality

Morality is a facet of absolute truth. Thus, relativists often declare, "It's wrong for you to impose your morals on me." By declaring something is wrong, the relativist is contradicting himself by imposing his morals upon you.

You might hear, *"There is no right, there is no wrong!"* You must ask, is that statement right or wrong?

If you catch a relativist in the act of doing something they know is absolutely wrong, and you try to point it out to them, they may respond in anger, "Truth is relative! There's no right and there's no wrong! We should be able to do whatever we want!"

If that is a true statement and there is no right and there is no wrong, and everyone should be able to do whatever they want, then why have they become angry? What basis do they have for their anger? You can't be appalled by an injustice, or anything else for that matter, unless an absolute has somehow been violated.

The World Is Filled With Absolute Truth

We all know there is absolute truth. It seems the more we argue against it, the more we prove its existence. Reality is absolute whether you feel like being cogent or not. Philosophically, relativism is contradictory. Practically, relativism is anarchy.

A Relativistic Viewpoint

A relativist maintains that everyone should be able to believe and do whatever he or she wants. Of course, this view is emotionally satisfying, until that person comes home to find his house has been robbed, or someone seeks to hurt him, or someone cuts in front of him in line.

No relativist will come home to find his house robbed and say, "Oh, how wonderful that the burglar was able to fulfill his or her view of reality by robbing my house. Who am I to impose my view of right and wrong on this wonderful burglar?"

Quite the contrary, the relativist will feel violated just like anyone else. And then, of course, it's OK for him to be a relativist, as long as the "system" acts in an absolutist way by protecting his or her "unalienable rights."

Whatever Happened To The Truth?
Linda Keffer of Focus On The Family

In our world today, the idea of ultimate truth — something that is true at all times in all places and has relevance for our lives — is about as extinct as the dinosaur. In fact, nearly three out of four Americans say there is no such thing as ultimate, or absolute, truth. And the numbers don't look much better among those who claim to follow Jesus.

In a society where ultimate truth is treated like a fairy tale, an outdated idea or even an insult to human intelligence, the motto of the day becomes, **"WHATEVER!"** Believe whatever you want. Do whatever seems best to you. Live for whatever brings you pleasure, as long as it doesn't hurt anyone. And of course, be tolerant. Don't try to tell anyone that their *whatever* is wrong.

But where does that leave us? If we have ultimate truth, it gives us both a way to explain the world around us and a basis for making decisions. Without it, we're alone. We're just 7 billion organisms running around, bumping into each other with nothing unifying to work for or believe in.

It's every man for himself. And we're without a purpose; if there's no true story of where we came from and why we're here, then there's nothing that really gives our lives meaning. Sounds a little depressing, huh? And maybe frightening.

Has life always been like this? Do we have to carry on this way? No! In fact, in the scope of history, *whatever* is a pretty new way of viewing the world.

When Truth Wasn't A Bad Word

If you consider that the human race has been around for thousands of years, the last two or three hundred don't seem that long. And it is in that short time that our beliefs have shifted from a certainty in truth to a denial that it even exists.

From before Jesus was born until the late 1700s, people believed in a spiritual or supernatural world that coexisted with the physical world, affecting all aspects of life. People who lived during that time also generally believed that the natural world was orderly, that it could be studied and that truth was touchable, based on supernatural rather than natural realities.

Those people gave spiritual explanations for what went on in their physical lives. They also made moral decisions on the basis of the supernatural; things were believed to be right or wrong based on what God thought. Of course, not everyone believed in the God of Israel, but history shows that every civilization developed a way of thinking that looked for truth in the supernatural world.

Societies that didn't recognize the one true God were sometimes closer to finding Him and finding truth than people are today because they were actively seeking these things.

That's what the apostle Paul found when he visited Greece. He walked into a group of scholarly Athenians and said, "Men of Athens! I see that in every way you are very religious. For as I walked around and looked carefully at your objects of worship, I even found an altar with this inscription: To an unknown god. Now what you worship as something unknown I am going to proclaim to you" (Acts 17:22-23).

Paul went on to talk about the real God, and many Athenians listened. They had not formerly known God, but they knew that there was something supernatural that they were missing. The altar they had built showed that they were looking for truth, so when Paul showed up, they were eager to hear about Jehovah — He was what they had been missing!

Another thing is clear about how ancient people looked for truth —

they watched and listened for signs of the supernatural within the natural world. Bottom line: They expected God to reveal himself through words and circumstances. *Revelation* was their source of ultimate truth.

So, How'd We Get Into This Mess?

Around the mid-1700s, common ideas about truth and the supernatural changed. At first, the new ideas weren't bad. People started focusing on the uniqueness of humans and the human mind. And they were right — we are unique and God has made us special. Unfortunately, the good idea took a wrong turn. Instead of praising God for creating our minds, people started treating the human mind as if it were a god.

Scientists made astounding discoveries, and the scope of knowledge seemed limitless. Charles Darwin had given people an excuse for forgetting God with his ideas about evolution and natural selection.

People began to think that maybe the world just happened by chance. And Sir Isaac Newton proved that the natural world is a big machine that runs according to a certain set of laws. If we could just discover these laws, then we'd know how to better manage our lives and thus improve the world.

But there was one huge problem with these ideas. Science can discover truth only in the natural realm. In other words, it works only on things that can be tested. Rather than admitting that our ability to discover truth is limited, we decided to say that reality is limited. People began to believe that the physical world is all there is — no supernatural world and no God (or if there is a God, He doesn't have much to do with us).

Since people no longer believed in the revelation of a supernatural standard, they had to find another basis for moral decisions. Their sources of truth were reason, facts and science, so it's no surprise that those same sources became the standard for moral decisions. Instead of asking, "What would Jesus do?" people asked, "What does reason tell us is best for humanity?"

What Happened Then?

Everything worked fine until we started coming up with questions and problems that science couldn't answer. It took nearly 200 years, but eventually people started to realize that science and reason hadn't eliminated the problems of poverty, crime and hunger. After a while, we became discouraged with trying to find a better solution and decided that there just isn't a solution.

Science isn't the answer; it isn't *the* source of truth. And of course, God had been excluded from the picture long ago. So what did that leave us? Nothing. Oh, of course, there are true statements that can be made about what we see around us: "I have three apples," "The law of gravity applies," etc.

But once we've excluded both God and reason, there's nothing left to provide ultimate truth — the kind of truth that is true always and everywhere, the kind of truth on which to base our moral decisions. And that leads us to *whatever*.

Living In A, "Whatever," World

If there is no basis for moral decisions, then *whatever* you choose to do is fine. Of course, most people like to believe that they have *some* basis for the decisions they make. So we've constructed our own standards:

- **Science And Reason**

  Even though most people have thrown out reason as the source of ultimate truth, some still cling to it. "If I can't see it, hear it, smell it, taste it, touch it and test it, it can't be true," they say.

- **Popular Opinion**

You only have to look as far as your TV to know that society thinks popular opinion is a good basis for making decisions. Otherwise, why would our advertisements tell us to "catch the wave" or make the "choice of a new generation"? All these ads appeal to the idea that "everyone is doing it" and that you should, too.

- **Feelings**

Emotions are perhaps the most popular basis for making choices today. After all, how can anyone argue with how you feel? If feelings are a good standard for decision-making, then you'll never have to come up with a better defense than, "I did it because I felt like it."

It doesn't take a lot of "what if" scenarios to realize that there are major problems with all these approaches to decision-making. What if you're asking a question that science can't answer?

What if the group changes its opinion? How do you know which one was right? And what if following your feelings leads you to an action with consequences you can't handle? We've gotten ourselves into this whatever mess, but it's getting harder and harder to live here. So how do we get out?

Recognizing The Need For Truth

The first rung on the ladder out of this "no-truth" hole is realizing that it's reasonable to desire truth. In fact, those who tell you it's useless or narrow-minded to believe in ultimate truth have more explaining to do than they can pull off. When someone says,

"There is no such thing as absolute truth," that person is actually making a statement that he or she believes to be absolutely true. Contradictory, isn't it?

And it's even reasonable to search for ultimate truth in God. Those who say there is no God on whom to base our standards have a very hard time dealing with these questions:

Why do we have personalities? If there is no personal God who "shared these bits of His personality with us," where did we get them?

Why do the pieces of the universe fit together so intricately? If there isn't a higher standard outside the natural world ordering the way things work, then why do they work so well?

Why do we have a strong desire for purpose and meaning in life? If there is no "big picture" that explains where we came from and why we're here, why do we ask questions about purpose and spend our lives trying to find the answers?

These questions don't automatically take us to the truth, but they do give us a place to start looking.

Where Do We Go From Here?

If you got lost hiking in the woods, what would you do to find your way? If you knew anything about outdoor survival, you wouldn't keep wandering around, trying new paths and hoping you'd eventually stumble upon the right one. Instead, you'd turn around and retrace your steps until you found where you went wrong. Then you'd make a better choice and go on from there.

In our search for truth, we are obviously lost. In fact, many of us have given up hope of ever reaching our destination. Those still looking for truth have chosen to keep wandering rather than turn around and fix past mistakes. But making that 180-degree turn and taking a hard look at where we've gone wrong in the past is exactly what we need to do.

We have already discussed the fact that through most of history, people believed in objective truth and the supernatural. And they believed that the two were closely related.

When these ideas got lost, it was because society made two distinctly wrong turns. First, people abused human reason and intellect. Second, they threw God out the window. If we are to get back on the right track, we've got to go back and fix these mistakes.

Fixing The Mistake

"Science And Reason"

It's important to remember that the use of reason isn't what destroyed belief in truth. The problem was that people misused reason, mistaking it for something much bigger and more powerful than it really is. Many have already discovered this wrong turn, but in trying to fix it, they've made another, equally dangerous, mistake.

Have you ever heard someone say that Christianity is based on ignorant, blind faith? Unfortunately, in some ways, Christians have earned that insult.

Many Christians today don't want to be like the people of the 1700s, who relied on reason instead of God as the source of truth, so we've put thinking on the back burner of our faith. But the human intellect is not a bad thing. God created our minds, and He wants us to glorify Him by *using them!*

"Situational Ethics"

Got\Questions.org

"Situational Ethics," the belief that what is right or wrong is relative to the situation. There is no right or wrong; therefore, whatever feels or seems right at the time and in that situation is right.

Of course, situational ethics leads to a subjective, "whatever feels good" mentality and lifestyle, which has a devastating effect on society and individuals. This is postmodernism, creating a society that regards all values, beliefs, lifestyles, and truth claims as equally valid.

A good question to ask people who say, "There is no absolute truth" is this: "Are you absolutely sure of that?" If they say "yes," they have made an absolute statement—which itself implies the existence of absolutes. They are saying that the very fact there is no absolute truth is the one and only absolute truth.

Beside the problem of self-contradiction, there are several other logical problems one must overcome to believe that there are no absolute or universal truths.

One is that all humans have limited knowledge and finite minds and, therefore, cannot logically make absolute negative statements.

A person cannot logically say, "There is no God" (even though many do so), because, in order to make such a statement, he would need to have absolute knowledge of the entire universe from beginning to end. Since that is impossible, the most anyone can logically say is "With the limited knowledge I have, I do not believe there is a God."

Another problem with the denial of absolute or universal truth is that it fails to live up to what we know to be true in our own consciences, our own experiences, and what we see in the real world.

If there is no such thing as absolute truth, then there is nothing ultimately right or wrong about anything. What might be "right" for you does not mean it is "right" for me.

While on the surface this type of relativism seems to be appealing, what it means is that everybody sets his or her own rules to live by and does what he or she thinks is right. Inevitably, one person's sense of right will soon clash with another's.

What happens if it is "right" for me to ignore traffic lights, even when they are red? I put many lives at risk. Or I might think it is right to steal from you, and you might think it is not right. Clearly, our standards of right and wrong are in conflict.

If there is no absolute truth, no standard of right and wrong that we are all accountable to, then we can never be sure of anything. People would be free to do whatever they want—murder, rape, steal, lie, cheat, etc., and no one could say those things would be wrong.

There could be no government, no laws, and no justice, because one could not even say that the majority of the people have the right to make and enforce standards upon the minority. A world without absolutes would be the most horrible world imaginable.

From a spiritual standpoint, this type of relativism results in religious confusion, with no one true religion and no way of having a right relationship with God. All religions would therefore be false because they all make absolute claims regarding the afterlife. It is not uncommon today for people to believe that two diametrically opposed religions could both be equally "true," even though both religions claim to have the only way to heaven or teach two totally opposite "truths."

People who do not believe in absolute truth ignore these claims and embrace a more tolerant universalism that teaches all religions are equal and all roads lead to heaven. People who embrace this worldview vehemently oppose evangelical Christians who believe the Bible when it says that Jesus is *"the way, and the truth, and the life"* and that He is the ultimate manifestation of truth and the only way one can get to heaven (John 14:6).

Tolerance has become the one cardinal virtue of the postmodern society, the one absolute, and, therefore, intolerance is the only evil. Any dogmatic belief—especially a belief in absolute truth—is viewed as intolerance, the ultimate sin.

Those who deny absolute truth will often say that it is all right to believe what you want, as long as you do not try to impose your beliefs on others. But this view itself is a belief about what is right and wrong, and those who hold this view most definitely do try to impose it on others. They set up a standard of behavior, which they insist others follow, thereby violating the very thing they claim to uphold, another self-contradicting position.

Those who hold such a belief simply do not want to be accountable for their actions. If there is absolute truth, then there are absolute standards of right and wrong, and we are accountable to those standards. This accountability is what people are really rejecting when they reject absolute truth.

The denial of absolute or universal truth and the cultural relativism that comes with it are the logical result of a society that has embraced the theory of evolution as the explanation for life. If naturalistic evolution is true, then life has no meaning, we have no purpose, and there cannot be any absolute right or wrong.

Man is then free to live as he pleases and is accountable to no one for his actions. Yet no matter how much sinful men deny the existence of God and absolute truth, they still will someday stand before Him in judgment.

The Bible declares

> *"what may be known about God is plain to them, because God has made it plain to them. For since the creation of the world God's invisible qualities—his eternal power and divine nature—have been clearly seen, being understood from what has been made, so that men are without excuse.*

> *For although they knew God, they neither glorified him as God nor gave thanks to him, but their thinking became futile and their foolish hearts were darkened. Although they claimed to be wise, they became fools"* (Romans 1:19-22).

Is there any evidence for the existence of absolute truth? Yes. First, there is the human conscience, that certain "something" within us that tells us the world should be a certain way, that some things are right and some are wrong. Our conscience convinces us there is something wrong with suffering, starvation, rape, pain, and evil, and it makes us aware that love, generosity, compassion, and peace are positive things for which we should strive.

This is universally true in all cultures in all times. The Bible describes the role of the human conscience in Romans 2:14-16:

> *"Indeed, when Gentiles, who do not have the law, do by nature things required by the law, they are a law for themselves, even though they do not have the law, since they show that the requirements of the law are written on their hearts, their consciences also bearing witness, and their thoughts now accusing, now even defending them. This will take place on the day when God will judge men's secrets through Jesus Christ, as my gospel declares."*

The second evidence for the existence of absolute truth is science. Science is simply the pursuit of knowledge, the study of what we know and the quest to know more.

Therefore, all scientific study must, by necessity, be founded upon the belief that there are objective realities existing in the world and these realities can be discovered and proven. Without absolutes, what would there be to study? How could one know that the findings of science are real? In fact, the very laws of science are founded on the existence of absolute truth.

The third evidence for the existence of absolute or universal truth is religion. All the religions of the world attempt to give meaning and definition to life. They are born out of mankind's desire for something more than simple existence.

Through religion, humans seek God, hope for the future, forgiveness of sins, peace in the midst of struggle, and answers to our deepest questions.

Religion is really evidence that mankind is more than just a highly evolved animal. It is evidence of a higher purpose and of the existence of a personal and purposeful Creator who implanted in man the desire to know Him. And if there is indeed a Creator, then He becomes the standard for absolute truth, and it is His authority that establishes that truth.

Fortunately, there is such a Creator, and He has revealed His truth to us through His Word, the Bible. Knowing absolute or universal truth is only possible through a personal relationship with the One who claims to be the Truth—Jesus Christ.

Jesus claimed to be the only way, the only truth, the only life and the only path to God (John 14:6). The fact that absolute truth does exist points us to the truth that there is a sovereign God who created the heavens and the earth and who has revealed Himself to us in order that we might know Him personally through His Son Jesus Christ. That is the absolute truth.

Most People Will Accept Absolutes

Compellingtruth.com

The question is truly not whether there are any absolutes but rather which claims of truth are absolute. People will generally accept absolutes in areas of science or mathematics, but tend to question truth when it comes to matters of morality. For example, most people would agree premeditated murder is morally wrong, yet what about in a society in which cannibalism is practiced?

Is morality therefore simply socially conditioned, based on "what works" or what a given community agrees upon, or is there a standard of absolute truth or morality?

Philosophically, people may disagree on what is moral or ethical, yet virtually all people agree on some system of right and wrong. Therefore, the natural question arises, "Upon what do we base our moral standards?"

Many religious systems provide moral codes or standards for their followers, yet the Bible presents a unique look at truth. In the New Testament, Jesus was asked, "What is truth?" by Pilate (John 18:38), the very man who approved the death of Jesus.

When Pilate asked this question, he was looking into the eyes of the One who claimed to be the way, the truth, and the life (John 14:6). Further, because God is perfect (Father, Son, and Spirit), what He says is true. This includes the Scriptures that are called God-breathed or inspired by God (2 Timothy 3:16-17; Psalm 19).

Absolute truth exists, as no other option is adequate. Many systems of "truth" or morality exist, yet only Jesus Christ claimed to be truth and proved it by His resurrection from the dead (1 Corinthians 15:3-11).

Absolute Truth is real. Those who deny it, reject it only on two points, Sex and religion. All other points are ok with the "Nay-Sayers". These are the folks that are liberal in their thinking. They want to be promiscuous desiring to do immoral things without consequences. These folks are also those that deny the true and living God so they can proceed with evil and boast in their darkened state of mind.

Scientific Knowledge

Institute For Creation Research

Scientific knowledge is not a collection of subjective opinions. Rather, it is a collection of explanations about objective reality that is based on observed or predicted phenomena. In addition, the explanation must be verified repeatedly to confirm that it correctly models reality.

As our technical ability to observe reality improves, we are able to increase the quality and quantity of our observations. Better-observed data challenge our explanations, some of which will no longer fit the observed facts. New theories are then formed and either verified or falsified.

While our scientific knowledge changes rapidly, the absolute reality that is being modeled has never changed. The scientific method assumes an absolute reality against which theories can be verified.

The nature of truth has been explored throughout the centuries but the concept that truth can be absolute has been under attack for some time now. Historically, biblical foundational beliefs centered American society even when external forces threatened a change in direction.

Due to its nature, particularly in the area of absolute truth, this theological grounding gave great strength and resilience to the nation. The truths that the founding fathers held to be "self-evident" are now generally seen to be relative and confusion has crept into society, with a particularly deadly toll on the moral compass of our world. (Carolyn De Gregory Towart)

We, as Christians, must above all else, hold biblical truth as absolute and live by every word every day, no matter what others think or do. We must not allow our moral compass to slip away or our eyes to shift from God to ourselves.

We must stand our ground demonstrating faith in all that we do. We must realize that God has hidden His absolutes in plain sight so we, who seek truth, a can see them.

Absolute truth can only be found in Jesus. He is the source of all truth and is the embodiment of truth. (John 14:6) He brings order out of chaos, peace out of confusion, love out of hate, and life out of death.

CHAPTER NINE

Building A Christian Mindset

A Perspective Is A Mindset. It's How You Think.

The perspectives mentioned are spiritual "Building Blocks". They will give you a mindset that will shape your thinking and change your reality. They are also hidden in plain sight. Only those who seek them will find them.

Each perspective is God sent and anointed so you can establish a way of thinking that honors your Heavenly Father and glorifies the name of Jesus. They are also "Spiritual Vitamins" that will strengthen your faith and shape your destiny.

All of the perspectives must be applied to your daily thought life in order to be of any benefit. Just knowing them will not accomplish any true mindset shift. You must take them to heart and live in them. Make Them Your *Confession of Faith* and they will keep you walking in faith and doing God's will.

I have presented each perspective as my own confession of faith. I look at them often and believe them with my whole heart.

I have noticed that this process has indeed caused me to walk in the Spirit, identify evil attacks and snares, and made it easier to discern the Will of God in my daily life. They are life changing for sure.

We will be discussing many different perspectives. Each perspective is a "Building Block" that, when attached to each other, form a Christian Mindset. Listed below is a listing of those perspectives. They are life changing. If you see one in the Scriptures that I missed email me and I will review it for future additions.

Here's my current list:

A "Can Do" Attitude	Finding Rest
Accepted And Loved	Finding Strength In Weakness
Agreeing With God	
All Things Work Together	Forgiving Enemies
Angels In Our Midst	Giving Thanks
Anger Management	God's Peace Decides
Attaining God's Direction	God At Work In Us
Being Accepted And Loved	Great & Precious Promises
	Growing In God's Grace
Filled With God's Spirit	Jesus Is Coming Soon
Being Happy In The Lord	Living By Faith
Confusion Is Anti-God	Opening Heavens Door
Divine Healing	Overcoming Evil
Divine Counsel	Rejoice & Be Glad
Doing My Best	Relief From Burdens
Don't Worry	Remaining In Perfect Peace
Establishing Your Thoughts	
	Renewal of Strength
Every Need Met	Spiritual Authority
Fear Is Not From God	Stopping The Reign of Sin
Fear of Evil Dooers	The Enemy

The Transformation Process	Where There Is No Way
Things Have Reasons	Removal of Personal Sin

Perspective #1… I Am Loved And Accepted By God.

What Other Folks Think Just Doesn't Matter. Read what the Bible says…

> *"For God so loved the world, that he gave his only begotten Son, that whosoever believeth in him should not perish, but have everlasting life."* (John 3:16)

Sometimes we get all caught up in what other folks think. We even, at times, strive to fit in by doing things we ought not to have done. The need to be accepted is a powerful strain on our well-being. Once we realize that we are accepted and loved by God, things suddenly change. What others think just doesn't matter.

We are free to live out our Christianity as the Holy Spirit directs. Having this mindset liberates us so we can soar like an eagle above all the negativity that life throws at us.

Perspective #2… The devil Is An Evil Spirit.

I will resist the devil and his influence at all times. Here's what Jesus said…

> *"The thief cometh not, but for to steal, and to kill, and to destroy: I am come that they might have life, and that they might have it more abundantly." (*John 10:10)

The devil is a real being and he is evil. Jesus refers to him as a thief that comes to kill, steal and destroy. Knowing this gives us a chance to defend ourselves. God will teach our hands to war and give us the weapons to fight the good fight of faith.

I Peter 5:8-9 tells us…

> *"Be sober, be vigilant; because your adversary the devil, as a roaring lion, walks about, seeking whom he may devour: Whom resist stedfast in the faith, knowing that the same afflictions are accomplished in your brethren that are in the world."*

The devil will use immorality, drugs, power, fame, riches or anything else he can find to capture us and convince us to do his will. If we know that he is behind a thing, we can protect ourselves before his kill, steal or destroy goals are accomplished.

Perspective #3...I Have Authority Over Evil Spirits.

The devil and all his followers were defeated by Jesus and now must obey our commands. Listen again...

> *"For the weapons of our warfare are not carnal but mighty in God for pulling down strongholds, casting down imaginations and every high thing that exalts itself above the knowledge of God"* (II Corinthians 10:4-7)

Evil spirits are real and they are bent on attacking God's children. They don't want us to manifest the fruit of God's Spirit upon the earth. (See Galatians 5)

However, they are not more powerful than Jesus who gave us the keys to His kingdom and said to resist evil and it will flee from you. (I Peter 5:8)

Thus we now have authority over evil spirits and they must obey us...as long as we speak the Word of God against them like Jesus did. He used scripture. Remember, the battle is for supremacy over your mind. Our bodies are temples that manifest good or evil.

Our weapons are such that we can cast down lies and imaginations. We actually dispel them by holding them up to the light of the knowledge of God that He has given us. We use the truth to dispel the lie. Thus…when we feel unloved, we take the truth of John 3:16 and speak it to ourselves until it takes root. We speak the scriptures.

Perspective #4…I Will Allow The Peace of God To Be My Referee In All My Decisions And Life Experiences.

> Listen… *"And let the peace of God rule in your hearts, to the which also ye are called in one body; and be ye thankful."* (Colossians 3:15)

This scripture actually encourages us to let the peace of God rule. The peace of God rules by refereeing every situation. He tells us when to proceed and when to back off. If you lose your peace, stop. If your peace remains, proceed. It's not rocket science. It's actually easy as long as you put God's will before yours.

Perspective #5… When I Am Confused, I Will Stop All Decision-Making Activity And Seek The Lord For His Peace And Wisdom. Hear this…

Confusion Is Not of God.

> *"For God is not the author of confusion, but of peace, as in all churches of the saints"* (I Corinthians 14:33)

Confusion is usually a result of going forward when you have no peace about the situation you are faced with. Realizing that your confusion does not originate with your loving Heavenly Father will shake you back into reality.

The sobering fact is… the source of your confusion is most likely YOU, because you did not allow God's peace to rule in the first place. The most important thing to remember when you are confused is to STOP AND PRAY.

Perspective #6… I Will Not Be Afraid Because *Fear Is Not From My Heavenly Father*.

I Can And Will Overcome Those Things That Frighten Me. Listen...

"For God hath not given us the spirit of fear; but of power, and of love, and of a sound mind." (II Timothy 1:7)

The scriptures tell us that God has not given us a spirit of fear but rather a Spirit of Power, Love and a Sound Mind. Knowing this assures us that when we fear, it comes from an evil source and we are to resist it in the faith and seek the Lord for protection. We are challenged to fight the good fight of Faith. "fear not" *("do not be afraid", "do not fear", "be not afraid", "Fret not")* is used over 110 times in the Bible. God is with us so why be afraid?

Perspective #7... *All Things Will Work Together For My Good.*

I Reverence God And Have Been Called By God According To His Purposes. That qualifies me for this promise. This is what it says...

"And we know that all things work together for good to them that love God, to them who are the called according to his purpose." (Romans 8:28)

All things mean all things, no matter how terrible they may be. It does not say that God sent them your way. He is not the enemy. He does no evil. However, He does work evil things together with good things in an effort to nullify the work of evil and ultimately bless you. Say it with me, "Things will work out because God is in the midst of that thing."

Perspective #8... I Will Not Let Situations That Are Beyond My Control Frustrate Me Or Get Me Angry. Hear Jesus again...

"Therefore I say unto you, Take no thought for your life, what ye shall eat, or what ye shall drink; nor yet for your body, what ye shall put on. Is not the life more than meat, and the body than raiment?" Behold the fowls of the air: for they sow not, neither do they reap, nor gather into barns;

> *yet your heavenly Father feeds them. Are ye not much better than they?"* (Matthew 6:25-26)

Considering that God works all things together for good, I can relax when things do not go my way, knowing that there is a reason for what is happening. I just don't see it right now. I need to trust in the Lord that He sees and is actively working in my best interest. Keep your cool and let God be God in your life.

***** There Must Be A Reason For That *****

Perspective #9... I will make myself ready because Jesus Is Coming Soon.

He Will Set Everything In Order And Rid This World of Evil. I Will Look For His Return And I Will Be Ready.

> Listen again ... *"He which testifieth these things saith, Surely I come quickly. Amen. Even so, come, Lord Jesus."* (Revelation 22:20)

There is no benefit in vengence or continual hate. Why?, because Jesus is coming soon and when He returns, He will set all things straight. Those that plot in secret to do you harm will be exposed in the light of God's glory to their shame. They will not get away with anything.

> *Dearly beloved, avenge not yourselves, but rather give place unto wrath: for it is written, Vengeance is mine; I will repay, saith the Lord.* (Romans 12:19)

That doesn't mean we can not defend ourselves from an attacker. It does mean that we, when wronged by another, should not take revenge or seek to punish them for their actions. That is God's job.

Perspective #10...I Can Relax And Feel Safe, Even Though Times Are Getting Worse Because *God's Angels Will Protect Me.*

Listen to the scriptures... *"The angel of the Lord encampeth round about them that fear him, and delivereth them. O taste and see that the Lord"* (Psalm 34:7-9)

The Angel of the Lord actually sets up his camp of warring angels all around you, that is, if you reverence God. Note: all Christians are called according to His purposes. He has called us unto Himself and for His glory.

However, not all Christians reverence Him. Some deny His Lordship, divinity, atonement and other fundamentals of the faith. The true nature of their beliefs is not rooted in Christ.

If we love Him, we will obey His Word and follow Him in this life. When we do this, He sends His army of angels to deliver us.

Perspective #11... I will confess my sins to God, knowing that He will forgive me and cleanse me from all unrighteousness.

This is what the Apostle John said...

"If we confess our sins, he is faithful and just to forgive us our sins, and to cleanse us from all unrighteousness." I John 1:9

Failing to confess your sins to God keeps you from His blessings... not because He rejects you but because you do not feel comfortable in His presence and draw back. It is called "Backsliding". When you ask for forgiveness, you acknowledge your faults and seek to repent. This pleases God and keeps you in His grace. Thus you proceed with a clean heart and a clear conscience.

Perspective # 12...I will rejoice and be glad that I am alive because God made this day just for me.

Read it for yourself...

"This is the day the Lord has made; we will rejoice and be glad in it." Psalm 118:24

The Lord has made the day…this is that day. What shall we do with it? We shall rejoice and be glad because He is in control of the day and not the evil one. When I decide to rejoice and be glad, I personify His love and glory in a positive attitude that gives me strength. It's all-good.

Perspective #13…I can do all things through Christ because He gives me strength to do so.

Listen to the Apostle Paul…

> *"I can do all this through him who gives me strength"* Philippians 4:13

When we are faced with adversity, hard times, weak faith, doubt, confusion and negative feeling, we can speak forth what obviously does not exist but can if we fight for it. The phrase is, "I can"… I can be happy. I can get well. I can love again. I can, I can… I can do all things through Jesus who gives me strength.

Notice that you do not confess or even try to do anything in your own strength. You focus on Jesus and His strength to get it done or get through the day or change from sad to happy. Your faith is in His power not you abilities.

Perspective #14… I will rest in the Lord, knowing that the battle is His to Fight and Win.

> Listen…" *The LORD will fight for you; you need only to be still."* Exodus 14:14

That was true for Old Testament saints and it remains true for us.

In a troubled world with uninvited experiences, it can get really hectic. However, if we know God, have seen His power in our lives and really trust in Him, we can rest from the worry, stress, fear, confusion or whatever.

REST MY CHILD

Rest, my child, sayeth the Lord
Take thy peace and be restored.
I have provided, thy mouth to feed.
From the beginning, I knew your need.

Do not worry, fret or even fear,
For my child, I am always near
To bless thy soul with love and grace,
To be with thee, face to face.

Come, my child, near to my throne.
Do not allow your faith to roam.
For those who will not believe
Can never find rest in times of need.

My Word shall see you through.
My grace I freely give to you
That you should rest, thy soul to keep,
Forever delivered from unbelief.

Written By
John Marinelli

Perspective #15...I will take counsel and daily inspriation from the Bible, God's Holy Word.

> II Timothy 3:16 says... *"All scripture is given by inspiration of God, and is profitable for doctrine, for reproof, for correction, for instruction in righteousness"* And...

> Psalm 119:105 *"Thy word is a lamp unto my feet, and a light unto my path."*

God gave us His Holy Bible as a life-long resource. We can draw inspiration, faith, hope and power for every situation. If you discount the Bible, you sign your own death warrant because that is where you discover the Christ of Calvary.

Perspective #16...I will strive to keep my mind stayed upon the Lord so I can remain in perfect peace.

> *"Thou wilt keep him in perfect peace, whose mind is stayed on thee:"* Isaiah 26:3

Remaining in perfect peace in a world of terrorism, political unrest, liberalism and the like is really hard. However, staying in the peace of God can be achieved. It takes only a consentrated effort to stay or focus continually on the Lord and His Will for your life.

The question is, *"What Now Lord"* Keep asking and He will direct you. You do not have to make decisions on your own. The degree of your success is equal to your dependancy upon the Lord.

Perspective #17... I will wait upon the Lord until my strength is renewed so I can soar with the wings of eagles, run and not be weary and walk and not faint.

> Hear it again... *"But they that wait upon the Lord shall renew their strength;they shall mount up with wings as*

eagles; they shall run, and not be weary; and walk and not faint" Isaiah 40:31

It's fun to soar with eagle's wings, run and not get tired and walk without being weary. It happens when we wait for strength, direction and power. It's only then, when we have a goal, a plan of action and a vision, that we can move ahead. It all comes to us from God so we can accomplish His will. Waiting is not so bad.

Perspective #18… I will seek first the Kingdom of God, knowing that God will supply everything else.

Here's what 4:19 says,

> *"But my God shall supply all your need according to his riches in glory by Christ Jesus"* Matthew 6:33 & Phillipians 4:19

Seeking the kingdom of God first is a matter of setting priorities in your life. Is He first or are you? Is He the source of your strength and very existance or is it something else? All must come from God. When He is in control, He supplies all that you need and there is no sorrow or torment attached to it.

Perspectivce #19………I will knock at the door of heaven, seek so I may find and ask that I may receive, knowing that God will open the door, hear my petitions and bless me with whatsoever I ask of Him.

> *"Ask, and it shall be given you; seek, and ye shall find; knock, and it shall be opened unto you"* *"And all things, whatsoever ye shall ask in prayer, believing, ye shall receive"* Matthew 7:7 & Matthew 21:22

We are instructed to *"Knock", "Seek"* and *"Ask."* God wants us to participate with Him in life's every moment. We are not a robot.

We are His children and He loves us and wants to bless us as we participate in His divine plan.

Perspective #20... I will trust always that the good work that God started in me will continue until the day of Jesus Christ.

> Phippipians 1:6 *"Being confident of this very thing, that he which hath begun a good work in you will perform it until the day of Jesus Christ:"*

We can easily get discuraged, feeling that we failed the Lord, our family and even ourselves.

The devil is known as the "Accuser of the Brethern." He will try to cut us down and shame us if possible so we give up on our dreams and visions from God. However, God has not forgotten us. He is still at work causing that initial work that He placed in us to come to maturity. You can trust in Him to bring it forth and keep it alive until Christ comes again...

***** Don't Ever Give Up *****

Prespective #21... I will acknowledge the Lord in all things and trust in Him that He may direct my paths.

> Proverbs 3:5-6 *"Trust in the LORD with all thine heart; and lean not unto thine own understanding. In all thy ways acknowledge him, and he shall direct thy paths."*

There is only one way to receive direction from God. That is... to acknowledge Him in everything you do...in all your ways. When you do this, you give Him control and crown Him Lord over your life. It is only then that He can lead you out of all the difficulties and bring you to the still waters where He can restore your soul.

Perspective # 22... I will not allow my body to be used as a instrument of unrighteousness.

Sin will not reign over my thoughts and actions. Romans 6:12-12 says...

> *"Let not sin therefore reign in your mortal body, that ye should obey it in the lusts thereof."*.

Body language is a big thing these days. It reveals how you feel or think. If you look hard enough, you'll see clintched fists, squirming torsos, rolling eyes and so forth. Then there are the vocals that scream out hate and nasty language.

However, we are the temple of the Holy Spirit. We are to reveal His character, one of Love, Joy, Peace, Longsuffering, Kindness, Temperance etc.

Our entire body, every member, is an instruments to sing the praises of God. To do otherwise would be treason against the Most High God. See the fruit of the Spirit and the deeds of the flesh in Galations chapter five.

Perspective #23... Whatsoever I do, I will do heartily as unto the Lord and not unto men.

> Colossians 3:23-24 *"And whatsoever ye do, do it heartily, as to the Lord, and not unto men; Knowing that of the Lord ye shall receive the reward of he inheritance."*

How many of us have seen others doing something for the applause of those around them? There are a lot of folks that give money, volunteer, visit the sick, do church work, etc for the praises of men. We are to do everything unto the Lord and with all our might.

A half-done job is just that. It blesses no one. But when we labor as unto the Lord, He becomes our boss and we rise to the challenge. Our work becomes full of passion and enthusiasm and without grumbling. That's the way it should be.

Perspective #24... I will not become a drunkard but will instead be filled wth the Spirit of the living God.

> Ephesians 5:18 *"And be not drunk with wine, wherein is excess; but be filled with the Spirit;."*

Being filled with the Spirit is a concious choice. It doesn't just happen to us. If it did, Paul would not have said for us to be filled. I realize that we receive the Holy Spirit at our New Birth and automatically become His temple.

However, demonstrating His character every day requires a submission to Him and a fresh infilliung or anointing. This is needed because our flesh wars against God's Spirit for control of our minds. The winner gets to reveal the good or evil therein…so we must yield ourselves to the Spirit and receive Him daily.

Perspective #25…I will not be conformed unto this world but instead I will be transformed by the renewing of my mind that I may reveal the perfect and acceptable will of God.

> Romans 12:2 *"And be not conformed to this world: but be ye transformed by the renewing of your mind, that ye may prove what is that good, and acceptable, and perfect, will of God."*

It seems that we are always in a struggle between good and evil. They fight for our approval and life applications. The World influences us with Power, Fame, Pride and, Riches. It says that we can have it all and be like God, a god unto ourselves. This is far from the truth.

The only way to escape its enfluence is to be transformed and that can only happen when we consiously renew our minds. How? By staying in the Word (Bible) and let it wash away bad thoughts, negitive actions and wrong perspectives.

Perspective #26... I will give thanks in everything: for this is the will of God in Christ Jesus concerning me.

> I Thessalonians 5:18 *"In every thing give thanks: for this is the will of God in Christ Jesus concerning you."*

God is so good. He is so kind and loving. His desire is to always bless us and not to harm us. He is worthy of our praise and obedience. It is only fitting that we give thanks to Him for all He does for us, even when we are caught in a trial or an evil attack. He will move mountains for us, making ways that do not exist if necessary.

Perspective #27... I will love my enemies and bless them that curse me and do good to them that hate me.

I will pray for them which despitefully use me and persecute me... that I may be the child of my Father which is in heaven: for He makes His sun to rise on the evil and on the good, and sends rain on the just and on the unjust.

> Matthew 5:44-46 *"But I say unto you, Love your enemies, bless them that curse you, do good to them that hate you, and pray for them which despitefully use you, and persecute you; That ye may be the children of your Father which is in heaven: for he makeshis sun to rise on the evil and on the good, and sends rain on the just and on the unjust. For if ye love them, which love you, what reward have ye? Do not even the publicans the same?"*

Very few people can forgive an enemy or someone that has otherwise hurt them. I do not advocate blind forgiveness.

Jesus said we were to forgive 70 X 7 but only when the violator has asked for it. I also feel that we do not have to stick around and hang out with someone who has a past history of offences. We should practice forgiving and going on to bigger and better things.

We forgive because our heavenly Father forgave us. That's what the children of God do…they forgive.

Perspective #28…I will not be overcome with evil but will instead overcome evil with good.

> Romans 12:21 *"Be not overcome of evil, but overcome evil with good"*

Doing good always overcomes evil because it blesses and builds up the one to whom you do good. On the other hand, evil can only Kill, Steal and Destroy. It will tear down instead of building up… but doing good restores what was broken.

Perspective #29…I will live out my life here on earth by the faith of the Son of God, who loves me and gave His life for me.

> Galatians 2:20 *"I am crucified with Christ: nevertheless I live; yet not I, but Christ lives in me: and the life which I now live in the flesh I live by the faith of the Son of God, who loved me, and gave himself for me."*

We are not to live this life in our own strength. We are to live it by the faith of Jesus Christ, the Son of God. To do otherwise is to miss the point of our very existence. We, as Christians, are all given a measure of faith.

This faith is God's faith. It brings hope, trust, expectations and power. Releasing it is easy. We simply let go of our lives and let Jesus take the wheel. We stand in His faith, not ours. His faith is written on the pages of the Bible in precious promises that become hooks to hang our faith on.

Perspective #30… I will take no thought of tomorrow, what I will eat or drink or wear because my Heavenly Father knows that I have need of these things.

> Matthew 6:31-34 *"Therefore take no thought, saying, What*

shall we eat? Or, What shall we drink? Or, Wherewithal shall we be clothed? (For after all these things do the Gentiles seek for your heavenly Father knows that ye have need of all these things. But seek ye first the kingdom of God, and his righteousness; and all these things shall be added unto you. Take therefore no thought for the morrow: for the morrow shall take thought for the things of itself. Sufficient unto the day is the evil thereof."

Worry is not cool. It strips us of our faith and binds us up with fear and confusion. The better thing to do is to not care about tomorrow, knowing God has it under control and will walk you into His blessings and keep you out of evil snares. When we trust in the Lord, we also rest in His grace and look for His provision.

Perspective #31... I will not be quickly provoked in my spirit because anger resides in the bosom of fools and I am not a fool.

Ecclesiastes 7:9 "Be not hasty in thy spirit to be angry: for anger rests in the bosom of fools."

Anger is a terrible thing. It can escalate quickly and often ends in violence. There is a good reason why we should not allow it to reside in our hearts. It's because the Bible says anger rests or resides in the boosom of fools.

Thus when we hang on to anger, we join the ranks of fools and miss out on the blessings of our Heavenly Father. Then we can not think straight and make poor judgements and mistakes that can be devostating to our future and fanily. A child of God should crush anger and cast it out of them when it raises its eugly head.

Perspective #32... I will declare and receive my divine healing from the Lord, knowing that I am healed by His stripes.

"But he was wounded for our transgressions, he was bruised for our iniquities: the chastisement of our peace

was upon him; and with his stripes we are healed" Isaiah 5:5.

"Who his own self bare our sins in his own body on the tree, that we, being dead to sins, should live unto righteousness: by whose stripes ye were healed. I Peter 2:24

Isaiah 53 tells us that our healing is in the wounds and bruises inflicted upon Jesus with the "Cat of Nine Tails" whip that was use to beat Him before taking Him to the cross.

This whip, the soldier's beating Him, and the crown of thorns cause the wounds and bruises. However, what man did for evil purposes God used to bring about healing to those who receive it. All that is needed is to believe it, confess it and receive it as your promise from God. All of this is based upon the premise that God wants His children well.

Jesus said in John 10:10 that His coming at that time was planned by God to bring "Abundant Life" to His followers. Certainly that includes wellness, not just partially but completely…physically, emotionally, spiritually, economically and every which way….so, call upon the Lord, receive your healing and don't let it go.

Perspective #33… I will believe God for things that do not exist, knowing that if He spoke them to me, He will bring them to pass.

"(As it is written, I have made thee a father of many nations,) before him whom he believed, even God, who quickens the dead, and calls those things, which be not as though they were." Romans 4:17

We can take great pleasure in knowing that our Heavenly Father is all-powerful. He actually calls those things that are not in existence as they were in existence. The Biblical example is with Abraham.

God said to Abraham that he would be the father of many nations. This "Fatherhood" did not exist, except in the mind of God.

If you read on in Romans 4:17-25 you will see that Abraham did not stagger at God's word. He believed it and held on to it and saw it come into reality. God will speak a word to us as well. Abraham was not the only receiver of a divine revelation. God's Holy Spirit will tell you things about you, your family and certain situations. You will know that what God said does not exist but you

will be challenged to trust, believe, confess and hold on to them, knowing that God is all-powerful and will, in His time, bring them to pass.

Remember, you do not call forth new cars, money, fame and other stuff. You call into existance what God has said to your spirit.

Perspective #34... I will not fret (worry) because of evil dooers.

> *"Fret not thyself because of evildoers, neither be thou envious against the workers of iniquity." Psalm 37:1*

We are all about worry, especially now that evildoers are trying to take over our country, turning it into a socialistic society with open boarders, imorality, and heavy taxation. But God says that we should not be worried...why is that? Because of what He said in Psalm 37:2

> *"For they shall soon be cut down like the grass, and wither as the green herb."*

When we discover that God is all-powerful and that He is on our side, there is no need to fret about anything. We simply trust in the Lord, and do good; so shalt thou dwell in the land, and verily thou shalt be fed. 37:3

Perspective #35... I will delight myself in the Lord at all times.

> *"Delight thyself also in the Lord: and he shall give thee the desires of thine heart."* Psalm 37:4

Do you want the desires of your heart? Well, start delighting yourself in the Lord.

The word, delight means, a strong feeling of happiness: great pleasure or satisfaction; something that makes you very happy; something that gives you great pleasure or satisfaction. The result of such actions and feelings is to gain the desires of your heart... not one but many. Delighting in the Lord is to be very happy that you are His child and love Him as He loves you.

Perspective #36... I will glory in my infirmities, knowing that my strength is made perfect in weakness.

> *"And he said unto me, My grace is sufficient for thee: for my strength is made perfect in weakness. Most gladly therefore will I rather glory in my infirmities, that the power of Christ may rest upon me."* II Corinthians 12:9

We do not glory that we are afflicted but we do glory that God has chosen to increase our strength in the midst of the infirmity. This action shifts our attention from the trouble to the solution and as we praise God, we gain strength to overcome.

It is not His will that we suffer. It is His will to equip us so we can be strong in faith. That's why we look for His hand in the midst of the trouble.

Perspective #37...... I will search out and claim the exceeding great and precious promises given to me by God so I can apply them and escape the corruption that is in the world and be a partaker in the Divine Nature of God.

> *"Whereby are given unto us exceeding great and precious promises: that by these ye might be partakers of the divine*

nature, having escaped the corruption that is in the world through lust." II Peter 1:4*

God has given us exceeding great and precious promises so we can join Him in His Divine nature and thereby escape the corruption of this world with all its lust. They are hidden in plain sight, left for us to discover them and apply them. They are great and precious. They are also in plain sight, written on the pages of the Bible.

Someone once told me that there were over 3,000 promises. Read until you find one of them. Then memorize it, study it and apply it. Each one will change your life.

Perspective #38... I will run to the Lord when I an burdened and heavy ladden that I may find rest.

> *"Come to me, all who labor and are heavy laden and I will give you rest. Take my yoke upon you, and learn from me, for I am gentle and lowly in heart, and you will find rest for your souls. For my yoke is easy, and my burden is light."* Matthew 11:28-30

Jesus said, "come unto me" and so should we obey…because He is the only one that can take away our burdens, restore our strength and cause us to really rest. If He will do that for me, He will do it for you as well.

Perspective #39... I will trust and hope in the Lord that I may grow in His grace and be fruitful.

> *"Blessed is the man that trusteth in the Lord, and whose hope the Lord is. For he shall be as a tree planted by the waters, and that spreadeth out her roots by the river, and shall not see when heat cometh, but her leaf shall be green; and shall not be careful in the year of drought, neither shall cease from yielding fruit."* Jeremiah 17:7-8

When God plants you by the waters, you have a continual source to help you to grow in His grace. You don't wither in the heat. Your roots will grow deep, causing stability. Your leaves will stay green even in drought…and you will yield fruit. This is a picture of an abundant life that is His blessing to all that trust and hope in Him.

Perspective #40… I will commit my works unto the Lord that my thoughts may be established.

> *"Commit thy works unto the Lord, and thy thoughts shall be established."* Proverbs 16:3

Unestablished thoughts are a breeding ground for confusion. When our minds entertain random thoughs, we become a playground for Satan. He generates evil thoughts and brings in negitive feelings. All of this brings our souls into bondage and takes us away from knowing the Will of God.

Dedicate your thoughts to coinside with what you know to be true from God, and your thoughts will become established or locked in as a rule of practice.

Perspective #41… I will look for a way when there is no way to be found, knowing that God will make a way for me.

God will always make a way for His children. Listen to what the scriptures say…

> *"And thine ears shall hear a word behind thee, saying, This is the way, walk ye in it, when ye turn to the right hand, and when ye turn to the left.* Isaiah 30:21

> *"Thus says the LORD, who makes a way in the sea, and a path in the mighty waters;"* Isaiah 43:16

> *"I, even I, am the Lord; and beside me there is no saviour. I*

have ... shall ye not know it? I will even make a way in the wilderness, and rivers in the desert". Isaiah 43:11

"There hath no temptation taken you but such as is common to man: but God is faithful, who will not suffer you to be tempted above that ye are able; but will with the temptation also make a way to escape, that ye may be able to bear it." I Corinthians 10:13

No matter what your situation is, God will make a way. When faced with a sea that is about to overwhelm you or the desert of dispare or temptation, God will be there for you to show you the way out.

He will even make a way where there is no way, just like He did with the children of Israel when they were caught between the armies of Pharoh and the Red Sea.

He made a way through the sea so they could escape on dry land. God is no respecter of persons. That means.... If He did such a thing for them, He will also do it for you.

The Greatest Perspective of All

Is Knowing That You Have Eternal Life
And Will Dwell In The House of The Lord Forever

There are many Christians that doubt their salvation. Some have told me that they can never really know for sure. Others put their hopes in a church membership or a particular religion. Still others tell me that they are good, never hurt anyone and this should qualify them for eternal life.

How can we know for sure? It is very important because this is the greatest mindset ever established. It is how you will think and act over the course of your life.

The Bible is the only source of truth that can be trusted. Here is where we turn to find help. Listed below are a few scriptures that will clarify how a person gets saved and why it is necessary:

Salvation is a gift of God.... *"For by grace you have been saved through faith, and that not of yourselves; it is the gift of God, not of works, lest anyone should boast."* Ephesians 2:8-9.

Salvation is offered to whosoever believes… *"For God so loved the world, that he gave his only begotten Son, that whosoever believeth in him should not perish, but have everlasting life."* John 3:16

Salvation requires repentance… *"I tell you, no; but unless you repent you will all likewise perish."* —Luke 13:3

Salvation can only be attained through Jesus… *"Neither is there salvation in any other: for there is no other name under heaven given among men, by which we must be saved."* Acts 4:12

Salvation is necessary because man has a fallen nature and is spiritually dead. This is because of sin. Hear what the scriptures say,

> *"And you has he made alive, who were dead in trespasses and sins:"* Ephesians 2:1

Hear some more about this…

> *"Wherefore, as by one man, sin entered into the world and death by sin; and so death passed upon all men, for that all have sinned."* Romans 5:12

> *"For the wages of sin is death; but the gift of God is eternal life through Jesus Christ our Lord."* Romans 6:23

> *"As it is written, there is none righteous, no, not one: There is none that understands, there is none that seeks after God. They are all gone out of the way, they are together become

unprofitable; there is none that doeth good, no, not one."
Romans 3:10-12

Man is in need of a savior and God sent His only Son to be that Savior. He died for us and better yet to live for us so we can live with Him.

"For if, when we were enemies, we were reconciled to God by the death of his Son, much more, being reconciled, we shall be saved by his life." Romans 5:10

So, what do you think? Are you in need of a Savior? Read Romans 10:10. It is with the heart that we believe unto righteousness and with the mouth that we confess our salvation. It's that simple.

"For with the heart man believes unto righteousness; and with the mouth confession is made unto salvation." Romans 10:10

Life's battles are fought and won…or lost…in the mind. It is not always what happens to you that causes the most dammage but how you react to what has happened. How you think is more important than what you are going through.

If you can develop a Christian mindset, it will see you through in times of distress. If you have a clear, more importantly, right perspective, you can overcome anything that befalls you.

As we read the scriptures, we see the "Hand of God" moving in the lives of those that believe and trust in Him. What we are seeing is one or more of these perspectives being applied to life situations.

If you believe and trust in the Lord, you will also see the "Hand of God" moving in your life. Just look for the perspective being applied.

I realize that it might be hard to memorize all the scriptures presented and to remember all the perspectives. However, you have to start somewhere to get somewhere.

I suggest that you start with these three building blocks:

>God's Peace Decides, Fear Is Not of God
>and Spiritual Authority ...

Then let the Holy Spirit lead you to three more until you master them all. The Apostle Paul said to Timothy back in the 1st century...

"Study to shew thyself approved unto God, a workman that needeth not to be ashamed, rightly dividing the word of truth." II Timothy 2:15

That's good advice for us today as well.

CHAPTER TEN

Hooks To Hang Your Faith On

The Bible is full of promises from God to His children. They are also hidden in plain sight. They speak of many things from healing to deliverance, salvation, forgiveness and a lot more.

The Lord showed me many years ago that these precious promises are really spiritual hooks that His children can use to activate their faith. We just need to find them and use them.

If I have a hook, or promise, and I hang my faith upon it, it forms a lifeline that holds me and keeps me in times of trouble. For example:

The devil seeks to deceive me into thinking that I am not loved. He brings around folks that criticize me, put me down and laugh at me. Like anyone else, I begin feeling down and worthless. Then I read,

> *"To the praise of the glory of his grace, wherein he hath made us accepted in the beloved."* Hebrews 1:6

Suddenly I see that God has freely given me grace but more than that, He gave it to the ones He loves…me. I now know that God really loves me and what all those other folks are saying are lies.

I hang my faith on the fact that He loves me and no other voice counts…thus I gain self-respect and self-worth. This is victorious living.

We will be looking at several hooks and how to hang our faith on them to overcome the attacks of the enemy and inward self-generated fears.

It is important to realize that there is a real devil that rules over principalities, rulers of darkness and Spiritual wickedness.

> *"For we wrestle not against flesh and blood, but against principalities, against powers, against the rulers of the darkness of this world, against spiritual wickedness in high places."* Ephesians 6:12

We are in a situation where we are being attacked every day. There is no neutral ground or safe city. We either fight back or fall prey to deception, lies and oppression. This is not a new concept or doctrine. Hear what Peter said to the 1st century Christians,

> *"Be sober, be vigilant; because your adversary, the devil, walks about like a roaring lion, seeking whom he may devour. Resist him, steadfast in the faith, knowing that the same sufferings are experienced by your brotherhood in the world."* I Peter 5:8-9

It's time to own up to the reality of a real enemy and learn how to fight back. We have precious promises in the Bible that guarantee victory over the sinister forces of evil. It's time to take back what we've lost and declare our freedom from future oppressions.

Hooks To Hang Your Faith On

As I have already mentioned, the hook is a Bible verse that is lodged in your mind. It got there from your reading the Bible and seeing the Divine Truth. It was so powerful that you could not help but remember it.

> *"Thy word have I hid in mine heart, that I might not sin against thee."* Psalm 119:11

It is our love for God that drives us to hid His Word in our hearts. We may not remember the address of the verse or the exact wording but we do remember the essence of what is being said. This is how a hook comes to be in our mind.

Let's look at a few hooks and see how they apply to our daily life. The 1st will be in relation to Salvation. We all have these nagging thoughts that torment us. They say, "Where did I come from?" Why am I here?" and "What happens to me when I die?"

Some folks answer these thoughts with Reincarnation. Others say, "You die and that's it". Yet other folks say you return into the fabric of the Universe that is ever groining and eternal. These conclusions are erroneous for sure. The only true answer comes from God and is found in His Holy Word, the Bible. Here's what it says:

> *"So God created man in his own image, in the image of God created he him; male and female created he them."* Genesis 1:27

We did not come from apes, a primeval swamp or a long evolutionary trek. We got here as a direct act of creation by God, Himself.

> *"So God created man in his own image, in the image of God created he him; male and female created he them."* Genesis 1:27

We are here to be the image of God in the earth…His likeness and image. This is our destiny and why God created us in the 1st place. Paul taught the 1st century Christians that God's image was the fruit of the Spirit.

> *"But the fruit of the Spirit is love, joy, peace, longsuffering, gentleness, goodness, faith, meekness, temperance: against such there is no law."* Glaciations 5: 22-23

> *"So God created man in his own image, in the image of God created he him; male and female created he them."* Genesis 1:27

Man was created male and Female, not male and male or female and female.

It was his intent to display His Glory in the earth through the lives of a male and a female relationship where love, Joy, Peace and all the rest of his character could flourish.

Same sex marriage is an abomination unto the Lord and a distortion of God's Glory. It was not why we were created and does not answer the question, "Why are we here?"

The final question is, "What happens to us when we die?" Jesus gave us the answer clear as day. John recorded it in his gospel letter to the church,

> *"For God so loved the world, that he gave his only begotten Son, that whosoever believeth in him should not perish, but have everlasting life."* John 3:16

Our destiny is to live with God for all of eternity. That's what will happen to us when we die, if we, as a, "whosoever", believe in Christ.

> *"We are confident, I say, and willing rather to be absent from the body, and to be present with the Lord."* II Corinthians 5:8

Where are we going when we die? To be with Jesus, the one we have believed in for so many years.

What's all of this have to do with hooks to hang your faith on? Simply this, the enemy of our souls is trying to steal, kill and destroy.

We, as sincere Christians and followers of Christ, know from the scriptures that we are God's creation, fashioned to reveal His image in the earth and destined to be with Christ when we die.

This truth forms a hook in our minds. It is this hook that we hang our faith on and thereby gain stability, hope, assurance, and peace of mind.

The placing of our faith on the hook is an expression of our belief. It activates our faith and brings us into a higher reality where the attacks of evil cannot hurt us.

No longer do we suffer the pain of a low self-esteem or the confusion of not knowing who we are and why we are here. The placing of our faith on the hook of Salvation grounds us and keeps us as we walk through life. To hang our faith on the hook is to believe the truth of the scripture with our whole heart.

Here's another hook that will bring you a clear perspective of life and keep you focused on the things that really matter.

> *"But he answered and said, It is written, Man shall not live by bread alone, but by every word that proceeds out of the mouth of God."* Matthew 4:4

There are many voices out there that call to us, telling us what to think, what to do and how we should live life. The liberal minded speak loudly as to immoral practices and lifestyle.

Others push a political correctness that is far from the truth of God's calling. Everybody we meet has an opinion as to what to wear, do or think. However, Jesus put it into perspective for us when He said we were to live by every word that comes out of the mouth of God.

God's Word clarifies and delineates. It sorts through all the voices and lights up those that speak the truth. We can hook our faith on God's Word, knowing that it will bring peace of mind, clarity of purpose and focus to our thoughts.

To live by the word is to hold up every thought, every voice, and every so-called truth to what the Word says to see how they fare. If they are not in line with the Word, they are false and can immediately be discarded as error, lies and deception. Thus we walk in the Spirit from Bible truth to Bible truth.

Using God's Word as a clarifying force, we can quickly identify many of the deceptions that other folks have fallen into.

All we have to do is say, "What does God's Word say on the subject?" Then look for what has been said. This is what Jesus did in Matthew 4:4. He said, *"It is written"*.

He had to have asked himself, what has been said before about this matter. He had already hidden the Word in His heart and could easily find it again when it was needed.

Now let's apply this simple process of holding everything in light of what God has already said on the matter to a few popular beliefs floating in our society today. What does God's Word say?

Reincarnation…*"And as it is appointed unto men once to die, but after this the judgment:"* Hebrews 9:27 Once To Die but never over and over again.

Same Sex Marriage…The Bible clearly condemns homosexuality as a sin and Christians who seriously follow God's Word must also condemn it as sin. Consider these words:

> Lev. 1:22, *"You shall not lie with a male as one lies with a female; it is an abomination."*
>
> Lev. 20:23, *"If there is a man who lies with a male as*

those who lie with a woman, both of them have committed a detestable act; they shall surely be put to death. Their bloodguiltness is upon them."

I Cor. 6: 9-10, *"Or do you not know that the unrighteous shall not inherit the kingdom of God? Do not be deceived; neither fornicators, nor idolaters, nor adulterers, nor effeminate, nor homosexuals, 10nor thieves, nor the covetous, nor drunkards, nor revilers, nor swindlers, shall inherit the kingdom of God."*

Romans 1:26-28, *"For this reason God gave them over to degrading passions; for their women exchanged the natural function for that which is unnatural, and in the same way also the men abandoned the natural function of the woman and burned in their desire toward one another, men with men committing indecent acts and receiving in their own persons the due penalty of their error. And just as they did not see fit to acknowledge God any longer, God gave* them over to a depraved mind, to do those things which are not proper." Christian Apologetics & Research Ministry

Sex Before Marriage... *Fornicators shall not inherit the kingdom of God.* I Corinthians 6:9 This term refers to those who engage in sexual activity, which God has declared sinful. He has not declared all sexual activity to be wrong. In fact, He condones and even encourages lawful sexual activity according to His design and purpose (I CORINTHIANS 7:2-4; HEBREWS 13:4).

Fornication refers to sexual activity outside of the marriage relationship between a man and a woman. It would include premarital as well as extramarital sexual relationships of whatever duration from a one-night stand to an ongoing affair.

Such activity was rampant in first century Corinth. It is rampant today in our own society. But it matters not how commonly it is practiced, it is still unrighteous and it will keep one from entering heaven. Christian Apologetics & Research Ministry

Abortion ... There are numerous teachings in Scripture that make it abundantly clear what God's view of abortion is. Jeremiah 1:5 tells us that God knows us before He forms us in the womb. Psalm 139:13-16 speaks of God's active role in our creation and formation in the womb.

Exodus 21:22-25 prescribes the same penalty—death—for someone who causes the death of a baby in the womb as for someone who commits murder. This clearly indicates that God considers a baby in the womb to be as human as a full-grown adult. For the Christian, abortion is not a matter of a woman's right to choose. It is a matter of the life or death of a human being made in God's image (Genesis 1:26-27; 9:6).

Pornography... Even though the Bible does not say anything about pornography, it is still wrong. Pornography deals with photography and/or illicit paintings and/or cartoons that are designed to arouse sexual passions in the viewer.

It is certainly possible that at the time when the Bible was written that there were various art forms that depicted sexually explicit things. But apparently this phenomenon was not sufficiently prevalent enough for the subject to be addressed in the Bible. Nevertheless, we can derive an accurate conclusion from Scriptures that deal with other issues and apply them to the issue of pornography.

> Matthew 5:27-28, *"You have heard that it was said, 'You shall not commit adultery'; but I say to you, that everyone who looks on a woman to lust for her has committed adultery with her already in his heart."*

> I Cor. 6:18, *"Flee immorality. Every other sin that a man*

commits is outside the body, but the immoral man sins against his own body."

Col 3:5, *"Therefore consider the members of your earthly body as dead to immorality, impurity, passion, evil desire, and greed, which amounts to idolatry."*

As you can see, the Bible tells us to be sexually pure. This is why Jesus even tells us to guard our minds. Note that He said in Matthew 5:28 that to even look on a woman lustfully is to commit adultery with her.

In viewing pornography, nakedness, and explicit sexual displays, lust is not only given the opportunity to rise but also most often lustful passions and thoughts are triggered in the heart and mind.

This is obviously sinful and clearly demonstrates that pornography is sinful. Add to this that oftentimes pornography involves viewing sexual intercourse between unmarried people and/or homosexual and lesbian activities and we have a very clear case of it being sinful. Even if the pornography does not involve viewing sexual intercourse between two people, it involves the viewing of naked individuals which is properly reserved for a husband and a wife.

Now someone may ask "What about art? It often portrays the nakedness of men and women? Why isn't that pornographic?" The difference between art and pornography is the difference between beauty and lust.

In art, the nakedness is intended to be a display of beauty and wonder. Pornography does no such thing. Its intent is to entice a person by arousing the person's lust.

But then, someone may say that they view pornography as an art form and that it is beautiful. But this is nothing more than an attempt to justify sin. Christian Apologetics & Research Ministry

Prostitution… Lev. 19:29 "Do not profane your daughter by making her a harlot, so that the land will not fall to harlotry and the land become full of lewdness."

> Deuteronomy 23:17-18 *"None of the daughters of Israel shall be a cult prostitute, nor shall any of the sons of Israel be a cult prostitute." "You shall not bring the hire of a harlot or the wages of a dog into the house of the LORD your God for any votive offering, for both of these are an abomination to the LORD your God."*

Judgment Day Will Come

Rape, Murder, Burglary, Adultery and Violence of any kind…are all included in immorality, which is not of God.

The Bible is full of scripture passages that condemn them and declare their punishment in the final Day of God's judgment. It's not ok to cheat on your spouse, steal from your workplace, take a human life, violate a woman sexually, or participate in any form of violent behavior. Those who do will face God's wrath one day and it won't be pretty.

All these things, when held up to the light of the scriptures, are clearly wrong and definitely not God's will for His children. Once we see that, we can stand in opposition to them and avoid the snare of the devil that has captured so many of our fellow believers.

Another hook to hang your faith on is Acts 4:12, the "One Way" theological truth.

> *"Neither is there salvation in any other: for there is none other name under heaven given among men, whereby we must be saved."* Acts 4:12

Jesus said, as recorded in the gospel of John,

> *"Thomas saith unto him, Lord, we know not whither thou*

goest; and how can we know the way? Jesus saith unto him, I am the way, the truth, and the life: no man cometh unto the Father, but by me." John 14:6

We know that the way to heaven is through Jesus and only Him. There is no path through being a good person or by believing in the church doctrines that promote religion as a way to salvation.

Jesus is the only way to God, the Father. Our destiny, hope of eternal life and very existence is in Him. To believe otherwise is error. Knowing this truth puts us in touch with God and full access to His grace and blessings. When we believe in Him as the only begotten Son of God that was sent as God's spotless lamb to be sacrificed on Calvary's cross for our sin, we find peace with God and realize the abundant life that Jesus promised. (John 3:16, John 14:6 &

Another Hook Is Romans 8:16-17…

"The Spirit Himself bears witness with our spirit that we are children of God, and if children, then heirs—heirs of God and joint heirs with Christ, if indeed we suffer with Him, that we may also be glorified together."

The central truth of Romans 8:16 is that God's Spirit bears witness with our spirit that we are children of God. We don't have to wonder if we are saved or if there is a God or feel like we are all alone in this world.

As we seek the Lord, pray to the Father and ask for guidance, it is the Spirit that communicates with us, telling us what to do, when to do it and how to act. He actually teaches our hands to war against evil forces. Over a period of time we will develop a history of things that the Spirit has done in our lives. It is this history that becomes the hook for us to hang our faith on.

I can go back in my Christian experience with God, now more than 60 years, and see the hand of the Lord in action on my behalf. It is the Spirit that moves the hand of the Lord in my favor. If He was there then, there is no reason why He will not show up now, when I need Him again.

One of my newest books tells my story. It is called, "Times Past But Not Forgotten." It's a walk of faith down memory lane where God showed up and helped me in my time of need.

Jesus said,

> *I will not leave you comfortless: I will come to you."* John 14:18

> *" But the Comforter, which is the Holy Ghost, whom the Father will send in my name, he shall teach you all things, and bring all things to your remembrance, whatsoever I have said unto you."* John 14:26

It is important to listen for the voice of the Spirit. He will confirm your birthright, destiny and resting place. He will walk beside you through every trial and heartache providing wisdom, peace, deliverance, and any other emotional or physical necessity.

Knowing that we are heirs of God and joint heirs with Christ is a powerful position to be in. It is worth all the suffering we may encounter as we serve the Lord. This perspective gives us automatic victory over fear, doubt, worry, and the fiery darts of the devil.

Another Hook Is Romans 8:28,

> *"And we know that all things work together for good to them that love God, to them who are the called according to his purpose."*

Here is a hook that is sure to work every time. It is, however, predicated on two things: 1.) You must love God. 2.) You must be in the "Them" crowd who are called according to His purposes.

All," Born Again" folks are in the, "Them" crowd. They make up the church. They are the "Whosoevers" of John 3:16 that believe that Jesus is the Son of God.

All, "Born Again" believers love God. We actually worship Him and adore Him because He first loved us and gave His only Son as a ransom for our souls.

So, do you qualify? If you do, you can rest assured that all things will work together for your good. It may seem like they don't but you do not see the overall picture as God does. He knows the beginning from the end and how to operate around man's free will to cause everything to work out in accordance to His will and in our favor.

We have a clear perspective in Romans 8:28. There can be no doubt. What we now are experiencing, good or bad, will ultimately work together for our good. Thus we can rest when we go through trials and experience tragedies and suffer loss. God is for us and is actively engaged in keeping us in His will and on the right path to Glory.

Hang your faith on this hook and you will find peace of mind, hope, a positive outlook on life and a deeper relationship with your Savor. I use a phrase when things happen. It reminds me of Romans 8:28 and that I should hook my faith upon it. The phrase is "There's a reason for that"

I have taken just a few of the Bible verses that are special to me to show you how the scriptures can be hooks to hang your faith on. There are many more promises, biblical truths and treasures to be found in God's Holy Word. You only need to search for them. They are, however, hidden in plain sight.

I would also suggest you read my other book, *"The Believer's Handbook of Battle Strategies"*. There are many more Bible verses that can also be hooks for the activation of your faith.

Remember, the times in which we live are full of terrorist attacks, fiery darts from the devil, critical judgments of us by others for being conservative, and attitudes of hate from the children of darkness. We must stand in faith, walk by faith and live in faith. Knowing the scriptures and believing them with all our hearts can easily accomplish all of this and more.

CHAPTER ELEVEN

Finding God's Will For Your Life

When I was a young Christian, I wished with all my heart that I could actually know the will of God. I often sent up prayers to heaven saying, "Lord, what do I do now?" It got so bad that I could hardly drive my car because I couldn't decide if God wanted me in the left or right lane.

Months went by with my continual prayers to God that shouted into heaven, *"What Do I Do Now?"* Finally, I was invited to a Bible study, started going to church and began reading my Bible. The answers came ever so slow but fast enough for me to digest and store them away in my heart.

Now, after 60+ years of Bible study, prayer and life-application, I can say with confidence that I do know and understand "God's Will" for my life. I am still learning and studying and applying. I even, at times, ask my self, "Why didn't I see that before now?"

I am going to open your eyes if you are blind, refresh your spirit if it is weary and strengthen your personal walk with Jesus, our Savior, by providing the tools needed to keep you keeping on.

Hang on! It's sure to be an exciting adventure.

Knowing That You Know

If you call yourself a Child of God, you should agree with me that you ought to know the Will of your Heavenly Father. You are openly admitting to a relationship and claiming family rights and access. Are we in agreement so far?

Knowing God is a logical assumption when we claim to be His child. Yet most of the Christians I know have serious doubts about the "Will of God" for them. This can only mean one of two things:

1. ***Your relationship with God the Father is not a close one.*** You pray, He listens, but you rarely feel His presence or hear His Voice….*or*

2. ***You have claimed to be a child of God but really are not.*** You know there is something not right but are too ashamed or afraid to openly admit to not being a child of God.

In either case mentioned above, there is a way to "know that you know" so there is no more doubt. However, knowing that you know takes Faith. God is speaking all the time through the Bible, through His Spirit and through other folks that He brings into your life. The quick fix to "Knowing That You Know" is to "Listen And Believe."

I can say, without a doubt, that I know the Will of God for my life. I can make such a claim because God, my Heavenly Father, has published 66 books that contain over 3,000 promises and many great statements as to what His will is for His children. It's all there in the Bible, just waiting for me to dig it out, "Listen And Believe".

To know that you know is a great feeling because there is no anxiety in it. I know and have been persuaded that this way is the right way and my new perspective brings me a lot of comfort, peace and hope for the future.

> *"And thine ears shall hear a word behind thee, saying, this is the way, walk ye in it, when ye turn to the right hand, and when ye turn to the left."* Isaiah 30:21

> **The Bible says**, *"For ye have not received the spirit of bondage again to fear; but ye have received the Spirit of adoption, whereby we cry,* **Abba, Father**. *The Spirit itself bears witness with our spirit, that we are the children of God: And if children, then heirs; heirs of God, and joint-heirs with Christ; if so be that we suffer with him, that we may be also glorified together."* **Romans 8:15-17**

As the scripture says, the Spirit of God will bear witness with our spirits that we are the children of God. If you've even felt, seen or otherwise realized the witness of God's Spirit, you will know without a shadow of a doubt, that you are a child of God.... and if a child also a joint heir with Christ.

How Does The Holy Spirit Bear Witness With Our Spirit?

Notice that the apostle Paul didn't say that the Spirit bears witness with our flesh, our souls or minds. He didn't say the witness would be through the intellect. He said the witness would be from ***Spirit to spirit***. That means it could be one of many gentle quiet assurances that we did the right thing at the right time. It could be a sense of stability when things are going rough. It could be, an "I just know" feeling.

The point here is that God's Spirit is talking to us and our spirit is listening and rejoicing that it can hear God when He speaks. One definite witness, that I can recall, is when I read the scriptures they started jumping off the page with new and fresh revelation. The Bible, all of a sudden, came alive and spoke directly to my spirit.

God's Holy Spirit was and is still confirming to me that I am a child of the Living God.

So we have a quiet assurance and a loud voice that calls us to the Word of God, where we receive faith, instruction, assurance, strength, and knowledge and a lot more. God's witness is everywhere.

It's Not Rocket Science

Finding God's Will is not rocket science. We have already learned that God's Holy Spirit is available to confirm or excuse our decisions in life. We also know that it is our," Free Will" that engages truth and activates faith to empower us to walk in the Spirit.

The key to *"Knowing That You Know"* is absolute submission to His Will. Here's what Jesus said,

> *"If any man will do his will, (God's Will), he shall know of the doctrine, whether it be of God, or whether I speak of myself."* **John 17:7**

We have to be ready and willing to do His Will. When we are, we will know the doctrine or revelation knowledge necessary to accomplish the revealed Will of God.

Question! Why should God give us the knowledge of His Will if we are not willing or not ready to use it? That would be a waste of time and energy on God's part and He just doesn't operate that way.

He has, however, already revealed His Will in the pages of the Bible. If we really want to know, we can read and discover and learn and apply all that God has for us. So, let's look at the Bible?

I will take you on a journey so you can discover some of the great and precious promises that prove out what the Will of God is. We will look at several scriptures and discuss them.

God's Divine Will As Revealed In The Bible

"And God said, Let us make man in our image, after our likeness: and let them have dominion over the fish of the sea, and over the fowl of the air, and over the cattle, and over all the earth, and over every creeping thing that creeps upon the earth." Genesis 1:26

God wanted to create man, (Mankind or Male & Female). His divine will was to create us. He did that in His likeness and image.

Then He gave us dominion over the earth and all its life forms. **What does this say to us?** Simply this, we were not a mistake, after thought or freak mutation of nature that evolved over millions of years. We were a specific, deliberate design to accomplish the goals and objectives of God in the earth.

"And let them have dominion" Genesis 1:26

The word, "Them" is all of us. We were to rule as the "Head" and not the Tail.

Now, let's proceed on our journey to discover the revealed "Will of God."

Revelation #1…God's will for our lives is to take dominion over evil and live in such a way as to reveal the image and likeness of God.

Man Is Created Male & Female

Genesis 2:18-25 is the biblical record of God creating Woman as a help meet for Adam. "And the LORD God said, It is not good that the man should be alone; I will make him a helper suitable for him."

> "And the LORD God caused a deep sleep to fall upon Adam, and he slept: and he took one of his ribs, and closed up the flesh instead thereof; And the rib, which the LORD God had taken from man, made he a woman, and brought her unto the man."

And Adam said,

> "This is now bone of my bones, and flesh of my flesh: she shall be called Woman, because she was taken out of Man. Therefore shall a man leave his father and his mother, and shall cleave unto his wife: and they shall be one flesh."

And they were both naked, the man and his wife, and were not ashamed."

Revelation #2... It is God's Will for a man to have a woman at his side. God ordained marriage and joined them together. Where does this leave Homosexuality? It was never in the will of God.

Revelation #3... God's greatest creation, (Mankind), fell into sin and is now in need of a Savior.

The Fall of Man

Death In Adam, Life In Christ
(Genesis 3:1-7; Genesis 7:1-5; 2 Peter 3:1-9)

> "Wherefore, as by one man sin entered into the world, and death by sin; and so death passed upon all men, for that all have sinned: (For until the law sin was in the world: but sin is not imputed when there is no law.
>
> Nevertheless death reigned from Adam to Moses, even over

them that had not sinned after the similitude of Adam's transgression, who is the figure of him that was to come." Romans 5:12-14

Romans 5:18-21 tells us,

"Therefore as by the offence of one judgment came upon all men to condemnation; even so by the righteousness of one the free gift came upon all men unto justification of life. For as by one man's disobedience many were made sinners, so by the obedience of one shall many be made righteous.

Moreover the law entered, that the offence might abound. But where sin abounded, grace did much more abound: That as sin hath reigned unto death, even so might grace reign through righteousness unto eternal life by Jesus Christ our Lord."

Man falls from God's reality into the darkness of sin. He lost the image and likeness of God, But, God still loves him and makes a plan for his restoration. Man is justified by the blood of Jesus and His righteousness was imparted to us, that is, all who believe.

Revelation #4…God loves us & does not want us to perish. Jesus said,

"For God so loved the world, that he gave his only begotten Son, that whosoever believeth in him should not perish, but have everlasting life." John 3:16 (Whosoever believes is given eternal life.)

"The Lord is not slack concerning his promise, as some men count slackness; but is longsuffering to us-ward, not willing that any should perish, but that all should come to repentance." II Peter 2:9

We must repent of our sin because Salvation is essential to knowing God's Will.

Revelation #5...God wants us to repent and accept Jesus as our Savior so we can live in relationship with Him.

> *"But God commend his love toward us, in that, while we were yet sinners, Christ died for us."* Romans 5:8

He died for us that we might live for Him. *(This is the foundation of the Gospel of Jesus Christ.)*

Revelation #6...God wants us to live life with a thankful heart. This allows God to be God over us and allows us to expresses our dependence upon Him. It also relieves us from the burden and stress of being our own god. We don't have to be in control of everything.

Give Thanks In Everything

> *"In every thing give thanks: for this is the will of God in Christ Jesus concerning you."* I Thessalonians 5:17

The Bible is filled with commands to give thanks to God (Psalm 106:1; 107:1; 118:1; 1 Chronicles 16:34; 1 Thessalonians 5:18).

Most verses go on to list reasons why we should thank Him, such as *"His love endures forever"* (Psalm 136:3), *"He is good"* (Psalm 118:29), and *"His mercy is everlasting"* (Psalm 100:5). Thanksgiving and praise always go together.

We cannot adequately praise and worship God without also being thankful.

Feeling and expressing appreciation is good for us. Like any wise father, God wants us to learn to be thankful for all the gifts He has given us (James 1:17).

It is in our best interest to be reminded that everything we have is a gift from Him. Without gratefulness, we become arrogant and self-centered. We begin to believe that we have achieved everything on our own. Thankfulness keeps our hearts in a right relationship to God, the Giver of all good gifts.

Giving thanks also reminds us of how much we do have. Human beings are prone to covetousness. We tend to focus on what we *don't* have. By giving thanks continually we are reminded of how much we *do* have. When we focus on blessings rather than wants, we are happier. When we start thanking God for the things we usually take for granted, our perspective changes. We realize that we could not even exist without the merciful blessings of God." (Excerpts from www.gotquestions.org")

Revelation #7…God is worthy of our trust and when we trust in, rely upon and adhere to His voice, He will direct our paths.

Proverbs 3:5-6 offers another "Will of God" Revelation.

> *"Trust in the Lord with all thine heart; and lean not unto thine own understanding. In all thy ways acknowledge him, and he shall direct thy paths."*

Why should we trust the Lord? Many Christians ask that question because of adverse situations they are in or have gone through. Here are a few reasons:

God is not a liar. He will always deal with us from a vantage point of truth.

God is immutable, which means, He can never change. He does not say one thing and do another. When He speaks... Well, listen to how Isaiah put it...

> *"So shall my word be that goes forth out of my mouth: it shall not return unto me void, but it shall accomplish that*

which I please, and it shall prosper in the thing whereto I sent it."* Isaiah 55:11

God is Love... This can only mean that He has no hate in him. His war and revenge is against His enemies who walk in darkness, steal, kill and destroy. His children are the *"Apple of His Eye"* and the subject of His grace.

God is our Protector... *"The angel of the LORD encamps round about them that fear him, and delivers them."* Psalm 34:7

God really does care for us... *"Casting all your care upon him; for he cares for you."* I Peter 5:7 *"Cast thy burden upon the LORD, and he shall sustain thee: he shall never suffer the righteous to be moved."* Psalm 55:22

God is a God of Blessings, Not Curses... (Psalms 1:1-3) *Blessed is the man who walks not in the counsel of the ungodly, nor stands in the path of sinners, nor sits in the seat of the scornful; But his delight is in the law of the LORD, And in His law he meditates day and night. He shall be like a tree planted by the rivers of water, that brings forth its fruit in its season, whose leaf also shall not wither; And whatever he does shall prosper.*

God is a God of Peace.... *"And the God of peace shall bruise Satan under your feet shortly. The grace of our Lord Jesus Christ be with you. Amen."* Romans 16:20

Because of who He is, we can, with confidence, acknowledge Him, trust Him, disregard our own feelings and follow His lead. He will always direct our paths.

Revelation #8... God's highest will is to bring us back to where

He had originally intended us to be, *in* His Image. Thus He speaks through the pages of the Bible, letting us know that He wants us to set ourselves apart for fellowship with Him.

> *"For this is the will of God, even your sanctification, that ye should abstain from fornication:"* I Thessalonians 4:3

The generic meaning of sanctification is "the state of proper functioning." To sanctify someone or something is to set that person or thing apart for the use intended by its designer.

A pen is "sanctified" when used to write. Eyeglasses are "sanctified" when used to improve sight. In the theological sense, things are sanctified when they are used for the purpose God intends.

The Greek word translated "sanctification" (hagiasmos [aJgiasmov"]) means "holiness." To sanctify, therefore, means, "to make holy." In one sense only God is holy (Isa 6:3). God is separate, distinct, and there is no other. No human being or thing shares the holiness of God's essential nature.

There is one God. Yet Scripture speaks about holy things. Moreover, God calls human beings to be "holyas" or holy as he is holy (Lev 11:44 ; Matt 5:48 ; 1 Peter 1:15-16). Another word for a holy person is "saint" (hagios [a&gio"]), meaning a sanctified one. The opposite of sanctified is "profane" (Lev 10:10).

The imperfect state of creation is a reminder that God's fully sanctified purpose for it has been disrupted by sin. Evil is the deprivation of the good that God intends for the creation He designed. The creation groans, awaiting its sanctification when everything will be set right (Rom 8:21-22 ; Rev. 20-21).

Human beings, made in God's image, were the pinnacle and focus of his creation. The sanctification of human beings, therefore, is the highest goal of God's work in the universe. God explicitly declared it to be His will (1 Thess 4:3).

He purposed that human beings be "like Him" in a way no other created thing is. Human beings are like God in their stewardship over creation (Gen 1:26-31).

Yet this role is dependent on a more fundamentally important likeness to God's moral character. By virtue of God-given discretionary autonomy (faith), human beings may so depend upon God that his moral character (communicable attributes) are displayed. (Dictionaries - Baker's Evangelical Dictionary of Biblical Theology - Sanctification)

We can never be holy in ourselves as He is Holy but by faith, we can become the very righteousness of God in Jesus Christ.

> *"For he hath made him to be sin for us, who knew no sin; that we might be made the righteousness of God in him."* II Corinthians 5:21

Revelation #9... God wants us to allow the mind of Christ to be in us and to join Him in humility, and servitude so He can highly exalt us with Christ.

> *"Let this mind be in you which was also in Christ Jesus, who, being in the form of God, did not consider it robbery to be equal with God, but made Himself of no reputation, taking the form of a bondservant, and coming in the likeness of men. And being found in appearance as a man, He humbled Himself and became obedient to the point of death, even the death of the cross.*
>
> *Therefore God also has highly exalted Him and given Him the name which is above every name, that at the name of Jesus every knee should bow, of those in heaven, and of those on earth, and of those under the earth, and that every tongue should confess that Jesus Christ is Lord, to the glory of God the Father."* Philippians 2:5-11

Revelation #10…God wants His Peace to Rule or referee in our hearts.

> *"And let the peace of God rule in your hearts, to the which also ye are called in one body; and be ye thankful."* Colossians 3:15

The word "Rule" in verse 15 actually expresses the intent to "Reign". It also can be interpreted as Referee as in a game. Paul is telling the church to allow the peace of God to referee any and all situations as though they were a game.

By doing so, you can use God's peace as a referee's whistle. It will blow with anxiety, confusion, worry and so on to let you know that you are off sides and in need of a reconnect with the Holy Spirit to attain His peace and sustain an attitude of thankfulness.

If you find yourself in anger, worry or any other such attitude, you can automatically know that you have lost God's peace. God wants you to walk and live in His peace so you do not have to experience all that jazz of the flesh. It will kill you if left unattended.

Revelation #11…God wants us to prove what is the good, and perfect will of God.

> *"And be not conformed to this world: but be ye transformed by the renewing of your mind, that ye may prove what is that good, and acceptable, and perfect, will of God."* Romans 12:1

We cannot allow non-believers to define what is or is not acceptable or perfect. We need to be the Bible that they will not read. We need to demonstrate what good is and what perfect is so others around us can see what the perfect will of God is.

The only way to get the job done is to reject the pull of this world into all its sin and be transformed in our minds so we do not fall for the wiles of the devil..

How do we renew our minds? By transforming your own mind from always thinking evil to allowing the mind of Christ to dwell in you. He will do the rest. Your mission is to not be conformed to this world but to align yourself with God's Will.

Revelation #12…God wants us to put on the whole armor of God so the devil can't hurt us.

> *"Finally, my brethren, be strong in the Lord, and in the power of his might. Put on the whole armor of God, that ye may be able to stand against the wiles of the devil. For we wrestle not against flesh and blood, but against principalities, against powers, against the rulers of the darkness of this world, against spiritual wickedness in high places. Wherefore take unto you the whole armor of God, that ye may be able to withstand in the evil day, and having done all, to stand."* Ephesians 6:10-13

Our fight is with the rulers of darkness. We are fighting because we need to defend ourselves. If we don't, we will become open game for the devil. Hear what Peter says in I Peter 5:8-9,

> *"Be sober, be vigilant; because your adversary the devil, as a roaring lion, walks about, seeking whom he may devour: Whom resist stedfast in the faith, knowing that the same afflictions are accomplished in your brethren that are in the world."*

Revelation #13…God Wants Us to Guard our Hearts With All Diligence.

> *"Keep your heart with all diligence; for out of it are the issues of life."* Proverbs 4:23

To keep ones heart is to guard it with all diligence. It implies that we should act as a gatekeeper that allows good things in and bad things from getting in. God wants us to protect our spiritual growth and resources. They can be depleted and even stolen by the devil.

Revelation #14… God Wants Us to Pray Without Ceasing

> *"Rejoice always, pray without ceasing, give thanks in all circumstances; for this is the will of God in Christ Jesus for you."* I Thessalonians 5:16-18

We pray without ceasing when we start our day talking to God and maintain an atmosphere of prayer all day. We rejoice and give thanks along the way and life flows along like a calm gentle sea.

Revelation #15… God Wants Us To Have Fellowship With Him.

Fellowship With God

> *"That which was from the beginning, which we have heard, which we have seen with our eyes, which we have looked upon, and our hands have handled, of the Word of life;"* I John 1:1

This simple and bold statement means that one can have a relationship with *God*. This idea would surprise many of John's readers, and it should be astounding to us.

The Greek mind-set highly prized the idea of *fellowship*, but restricted to men among men - the idea of such an intimate relationship with God was revolutionary.

Jesus started the same kind of revolution among the Jews when He invited men to address God as *Father* (Matthew 6:9). We really can have a living, breathing relationship with God the Father, and with Jesus Christ. He can be, not only our Savior, but also our counselor and our closest friend.

Actually, for many people this is totally unappealing. Sometimes it is because they don't know who God is, and an invitation to a personal relationship with God is about as attractive to them as telling an eighth-grader they can have a personal relationship with the assistant principal. But when we know the greatness, the goodness, and the glory of God, we want to have a relationship with Him.

Other people turn from this relationship with God because they feel so distant from Him. They want a relationship with God, but feel so disqualified, so distant. They need to know what God has done to make this kind of relationship possible.

John identified this eternally existent being, who was physically present with John and others as **the Word of Life**. This is the same *Logos* spoken of in John 1:1.

The idea of the *Logos* - of the **Word** - was important for John and for the Greek and Jewish worlds of his day. For the Jew, God was often referred to as *the Word* because they knew God perfectly revealed Himself in His Word. For the Greek, their philosophers had spoken for centuries about the *Logos* - the basis for organization and intelligence in the universe, the ultimate reason that controls all things.

It is as if John said to everyone, "This *Logos* you have been talking about and writing about for centuries - well, we have heard Him, seen Him, studied Him, and touched Him. Let me now tell you about Him."

This life was manifested, meaning that it was made actually and physically real. John testified as an eyewitness (we have seen, and bear witness, and declare to you) that this was the case. This was no fairy tale, no "Once upon a time" story. This was real, and John tells us about it as an eyewitness. (Excerpts from *David Guzik article on Fellowship With God)*

Revelation #16...God Wants Us To Seek His Kingdom First, Above All Else In life.

"But seek ye first the kingdom of God, and his righteousness; and all these things shall be added unto you." Matthew 6:33

Jesus said to seek first the kingdom of God in His Sermon on the Mount (Matthew 6:33). The verse's meaning is as direct as it sounds. We are to seek the things of God as a priority over the things of the world. Primarily, it means we are to seek the salvation that is inherent in the kingdom of God because it is of greater value than all the world's riches.

Does this mean that we should neglect the reasonable and daily duties that help sustain our lives? Certainly not. But for the Christian, there should be a difference in attitude toward them. If we are taking care of God's business as a priority—seeking His salvation, living in obedience to Him, and sharing the good news of the kingdom with others—then He will take care of our business as He promised—and if that's the arrangement, where is worrying?

But how do we know if we're truly seeking God's kingdom first? There are questions we can ask ourselves. "Where do I primarily spend my energies?

Is all my time and money spent on goods and activities that will certainly perish, or in the services of God—the results of which live on for eternity?" Believers who have learned to truly put God first may then rest in this holy dynamic: *"...and all these things will be given to you as well."*

God has promised to provide for His own, supplying every need (Philippians 4:19), but His idea of what we need is often different from ours, and His timing will only occasionally meet our expectations.

A growing number of false teachers are gathering followers under the message "God wants you to be rich!" But that philosophy is not the counsel of the Bible. It is certainly not the counsel of Matthew 6:33, which is not a formula for gaining wealth. It is a description of how God works. Jesus taught that our focus should be away from this world—its status and its lying allurements—and placed upon the things of God's kingdom. (Excerpts from gotquestions?org)

Matthew 6:33 is a call to priorities. We are invited to have fellowship with Christ but not in the appetites of sinful flesh. He wants us to walk with Him in His kingdom. Jesus says that if we sell out to Him, He will provide for us but if our selling out is to get rich, we have missed it before we start. God certainly wants us to prosper and be in good health but not by manipulation or exultation of self.

Revelation #17...God wants us to be filled with His Holy Spirit

"And be not drunk with wine, wherein is excess; but be filled with the Spirit; Speaking to yourselves in psalms and hymns and spiritual songs, singing and making melody in your heart to the Lord;" Ephesians 5:18-19

This scripture clearly reveals God's Will for His Followers: Don't get drunk, Be Filled and Sing. I want to focus more closely on being filled with the Spirit. I am sure you will agree that he is not referring to the spirit of evil or the human spirit of which we are already absorbed. It is obvious that the Spirit we need to be filled with is none other than the Spirit of The Lord.

How does one get filled with God's Spirit? The text here uses Greek words that mean to be continually filled as though it were possible to use up the Spirit and find yourself to be empty. I think that many Christians are running on empty and are in serious need of a fill-up.

Paul wrote: "Do not get drunk on wine, which leads to debauchery. Instead, be filled with the Spirit." In the original Greek, the phrase "be filled: is a present-tense verb.

To signify a "one-time filling," Paul would have used the past tense or a future verb tense; instead, he chose the present tense to denote that the filling of the.

The word Holy Spirit is not a one-time event, but a continual experience. Scripture says that we must be continually filled with the Spirit, not just once or twice filling seems awkward when referring to the Holy Spirit's entrance into our lives. The Spirit of God is not a liquid, like water.

He does not fill a person the way cold milk fills a cup. The Holy Spirit is God—He is one in essence with the Father and the Son—but He is also a distinct personality and has all the attributes thereof. That is why we refer to the Holy Spirit as the third person of the Trinity. Many Scripture passages point to these facts.

Like a person, the Holy Spirit searches, helps and guides. He knows; He feels; He wills. Scripture speaks of the Holy Spirit's mind, His love and His instruction.

In Ephesians 4:30, Paul wrote:

> *"Do not grieve the Holy Spirit of God, with whom you were sealed for the day of redemption."*

The only way we can grieve someone is if the one we are grieving has feelings.

Because the Holy Spirit is a personality, it makes more sense to talk about the Holy Spirit's control or compulsion in our lives, rather than His filling of our lives. Holy Spirit-driven is a good way to look at our response to His control.

A Spirit-driven person allows the Holy Spirit to direct and guide every decision. Because the world, the flesh and the devil oppose the Spirit-controlled lifestyle, we need to be filled and renewed continually. (Excerpts taken from Joel Comiskey's article CBN. org.)

Baptism with the Holy Spirit or in the Holy Spirit in Christian theology is a term describing baptism (washing or immersion) in or with the Spirit of God and is frequently associated with the bestowal of spiritual gifts and empowerment for Christian ministry. (Acts 1:5,8)

To illustrate, consider this…if we drank water from a glass, then the water would be inside us. However, if we went to the beach and stepped into the ocean, then we would be in the water.

We receive, as it were, a drink of the Holy Spirit when we are saved, but when we are baptized in the Spirit, it is as if that initial drink becomes an ocean that completely surrounds us.

Just as the indwelling Spirit that Christians receive when they are saved reproduces the life of Jesus, so the outpoured, or baptizing, Spirit reproduces the ministry of Jesus, including miracles and healings.

When Jesus gave the Great Commission (Matthew 28:19-20), He knew that His disciples could not fulfill it in their own power. Therefore, He had a special gift in store for them:

It was His plan to give them the same power that He had -- the power of the Spirit of God. So, immediately after giving them the Great Commission, Jesus commanded his disciples not to leave Jerusalem, but to wait for what the Father promised, "which," He said,

"you heard of from Me; for John baptized with water, but you shall be baptized with the Holy Spirit not many days from now" (Acts 1:4-5).

He further promised:

> *"You shall receive power when the Holy Spirit has come upon you; and you shall be My witnesses both in Jerusalem,*

and in all Judea and Samaria, and even to the remotest part of the earth" (Acts 1:8).

The disciples waited in Jerusalem as Jesus had commanded, and one day when they were all together,

"suddenly there came from heaven a noise like a violent, rushing wind, and it filled the whole house where they were sitting. And there appeared to them tongues as of fire distributing themselves, and they rested on each one of them. And they were filled with the Holy Spirit and began to speak with other tongues, as the Spirit was giving them utterance" (Acts 2:3,4).

Then Peter explained to the crowd that gathered that they were seeing the working of God's Spirit and told them about Jesus.

The Christian church began that day with the disciples and the three thousand people who joined them as a result of the day's events.

We can undertake making disciples of all nations with some degree of success without the baptism in the Holy Spirit, but when we do, we are undertaking a supernatural task with limited power.

It is God's will -- it is His commandment -- that we be baptized with and continually filled with the Holy Spirit:

"Be filled with the Spirit" (Ephesians 5:18).

The knowledge and reality of the empowering Spirit enables us to reproduce the works of Jesus. (Excerpts from CBN.org)

So, as I see it, the baptism of the Spirit is given so the believer can receive ministry gifts to aid in his or her service to the lord.

The In-filling of the Spirit is to replenish the refreshing required to continue day to day. One has to do with reaching out to others. The other has to do with hearing and fellowshipping with God so we have direction, purpose and a clear focus.

Revelation #18… God Wants Us to Know That He Is Working Everything Together For Good.

Why should we Trust God, Give Thanks, Pray Without Ceasing, and follow all the other teachings of Jesus? I would venture to say because of Romans 8:28 ,

> *" And we know that all things work together for good to them that love God, to them who are the called according to his purpose."*

God's Will is clearly revealed but only accomplished in the lives of those that Love God and are the called according to His purposes. We also know that God calls everyone to repentance and salvation (John 3:16)

The next pre-qualifier is that we love God. You would think that His children love their father. If they do not, it's because they do not know Him. In any event, loving God is the prime directive… Jesus said,

> *"And thou shalt love the Lord thy God with all thy heart, and with all thy soul, and with all thy mind, and with all thy strength: this is the first commandment."* Mark 12:30

I am sure you will see even more scriptures that will reveal the "Will of God" for your life as you keep reading the Bible. I have listed some more prominent ones so you can get a feel for what to look for as you read.

So far we have discovered 18 that should be active in our lives today. These revelation truths are as follows:

- God's will for our lives is to take dominion over evil

and live in such a way as to reveal the image and likeness of God.

- It is God's Will for a man to have a woman at his side.
- God's greatest creation, (Mankind), fell into sin and is now in need of a Savior.
- God loves us and does not want us to perish.
- God wants us to repent and accept Jesus as our Savior so we can live in relationship with Him.
- God wants us to live life with a thankful heart.
- God is worthy of our trust and when we trust in, rely upon and adhere to His voice, He will direct our paths.
- God's highest will is to bring us back to where He had originally intended us to be, in His Image. Thus He speaks through the pages of the Bible, letting us know that He wants us to set ourselves apart for fellowship with Him.
- God wants us to allow the mind of Christ to be in us and to join Him in humility, and servitude so He can highly exalt us with Christ.
- God wants His Peace to Rule or referee in our hearts.
- God wants us to prove what is the good, and perfect will of God.
- God wants us to put on the whole armor of God so the devil can't hurt us.
- God Wants Us to Guard Our Hearts With All Diligence.
- God Wants Us to Pray Without Ceasing
- God Wants Us To Have Fellowship With Him.
- God Wants Us To Seek His Kingdom First, Above All Else In life.
- God wants us to be filled with His Holy Spirit

- God Wants Us to Know That He Is Working Everything Together For Good.

The best way to find God's Will for your life is not to ask friends, family, or anyone else. They are not God and often are wrong in their own decisions, which, if I am right, will show up in their lives as a testimony against them.

The best way to know God's Will is to ask God in prayer, stay in the Bible and look for direction, correction and guidance. It's all there, hidden in plain sight. If you start a log of scripture verses and what they specifically meant to you, you'll have a history to refer to when you feel lost or confused.

"All scripture is given by inspiration of God, and is profitable for doctrine, for reproof, for correction, for instruction in righteousness" II Timothy 3:16

The Best way to live in this world is to apply the scriptures and live in them moment by moment. The truth you find in the scriptures will far exceed what this world has to offer.

CHAPTER TWELVE

Final Authority Believe It or Not

Let's talk about the Bible. I use it as my main source to validate all that I say. But most people, including Christians, do not read the Bible with any regularity and therefore do not know the God of the Bible. They know only what their pastor or others tell them.

The Bible is full of divine truth. It is like a field that has gold just lying on top of the ground. It is hidden in plain sight just waiting for someone to pass by and discover it.

Here's a brief history lesson.

The history of the Bible starts with a phenomenal account, the creation of all things. It's not one book like many think -- It's an ancient collection of writings, comprised of 66 separate books, written over approximately 1,600 years, by at least 40 different authors.

The Old Testament contains 39 books written from approximately 1500 BC to 400 BC, and the New Testament contains 27 books written from approximately 40 to 90 AD.

The Jewish Bible (*Tanakh*) is the same as the Christian Old Testament, except for its book arrangement. The original Old Testament was written mainly in Hebrew, with some Aramaic, while the original New Testament was written in common Greek.

Starting in about 40 AD, and continuing to about 90 AD, the eyewitnesses to the life of Jesus, including Matthew, Mark, Luke, John, Paul, James, Peter and Jude, wrote the Gospels which were letters and books that eventually became the Bible's New Testament.

These authors quote from 31 books of the Old Testament. They widely circulated their material so that by about 150 AD, early Christians were referring to the entire set of writings as the "New Covenant."

During the 200s AD, the original writings were translated from Greek into Latin, Coptic (Egypt) and Syriac (Syria), and widely disseminated as "Inspired Scripture" throughout the Roman Empire and beyond.

In 397 AD, in an effort to protect the scriptures from various heresies and offshoot religious movements, the current 27 books of the New Testament were formally and finally confirmed and "canonized" in the Synod of Carthage.

What I hope you will see from this snapshot of the Bible in history is that God took great pains to validate His Word to man over many years, keeping it clear, and indisputable as the only true source of His revelation. These eyewitness accounts and prophetic revelations all connect to make a complete proof of God's existence, character, power, love, salvation, judgment, compassion, mercy and forgiveness. His entire plan of salvation and things to come are all written down so we could benefit from them.

Time and time again I have asked the Lord questions and found the answers in the Bible.

I can remember one in particular. I was attending a small Christian fellowship that met in a barn. The leaders were teaching that God's judgment upon America was to come soon and that they could escape it by leaving the states and going to a remote desert-like place in another country. Several families had already moved to this undisclosed location.

I was a very young believer and not as knowledgeable as I am now in the scriptures…so I turned to Jesus and asked Him if these people were correct and if I should go with them. Here's what I read during my prayer and Bible reading.

> **Matthew 24:26** *Wherefore if they shall say unto you, Behold, he is in the desert; go not forth: behold, he is in the secret chambers; believe it not.*

This is just one example of many that God has communicated to me through the Bible. Try it…when you are troubled, confused or worried about life or just need an answer to life's never ending questions. Pray and ask Jesus to show you in His Word, the Bible. Psalms is a great place to start.

The Bible was written under "Inspiration" from the Holy Spirit. The word, "inspire" means "To breathe upon or into something". God revealed Himself through individuals who penned the written word.

As a young Christian, I often witnessed to un-believers, using the Bible as my source. Some of those I talked to told me that the Bible was not a source they would believe.

I went to my pastor and asked him what I should do because folks were not open to hear what the Bible had to say. He led me to Hebrews 4:12 and said. "Use it anyway," for the reasons stated in chapter four. Listen to what it says.

> *"For the word of God is quick, and powerful, and sharper than any two-edged sword, piercing even to the dividing asunder of soul and spirit, and of the joints and marrow,*

and is a discerner of the thoughts and intents of the heart." (Hebrews 4:12)

I did just that and began to see the words of the Bible break down barriers and soften hearts.

I know that anyone who is really seeking God and wants to know about Jesus will find everything in the Bible. Words will leap off the page, bringing fresh revelation, historical facts, wisdom, divine counsel and victory over life's every trial. All you have to do is spend some time every day in prayer and Bible reading.

THE STEPS OF A GOOD MAN

The steps of a good man
Are ordered by the Lord.
He leads us by still waters
Until our souls are restored.

Our pain and suffering
Are all taken away.
Replaced with great hope
For a brand new day.

He orders our steps
By Holy Spirit's breath,
That we may overcome
Satan, Sin and Death.

The steps of a good man,
Are not entirely his own.
They're given by God
So he doesn't walk alone.

Written By
John Marinelli

CHAPTER THIRTEEN

Free Will And The Sovereignty of God Believe It or Not

Am I in control of my own destiny or is it all planned out already and I am just a pawn in a much larger scheme? Sometimes I feel like I have no control over my life. Do you feel that way? The issue is of "Free Will" verses the Sovereignty of God. This has been a source of controversy in the church for centuries. Is God in control or not?

The **Sovereignty of God** is the Biblical teaching that all things are under God's rule and control, and that nothing happens without His direction. God works, not just some things, but all things, according to the counsel of His own will (see Eph. 1:11).

His purposes are all-inclusive and never thwarted (see Isa. 46:11); nothing takes Him by surprise. The sovereignty of God is not merely that God has the power and right to govern all things, but that He does so, always and without exception. In other words, God is not merely sovereign in principle, but sovereign in practice.

"Although the sovereignty of God is universal and absolute, it is not the sovereignty of blind power. It is coupled with infinite wisdom, holiness, and love. This doctrine, when properly understood, is a most comforting and reassuring one.

Who would not prefer to have his or her affairs in the hands of a

God of infinite power, wisdom, holiness and love, rather than to have them left to fate, or chance, or irrevocable natural law, or to shortsighted and perverted self? Those who reject God's sovereignty should consider what alternatives they have left." Loraine Boettner.

God created all beings including the angels but some have fallen. Let us be sure that this does not make God the author of sin, for, as man, they fell from their created state. This includes all false gods. But God is over them, whether they be angels, demons, or the god of this world, the devil.

The Psalmist said,

> *"Thou are exalted far above all gods",* Psalm 97:9,

And again, *"Our Lord is above all gods,"* Psalm 135.5,

And also, *"O give thanks unto the God of gods."* Psalm 136.2.

Man may fight against God but he cannot win. He often uses evil men to accomplish His will in the battle. Read about it in the next few paragraphs.

Jesus is said to have been slain from the foundation of the world, and the cross is one of the most credible evidences of Gods Sovereignty.

"Crucify him," "Crucify him", was their cry, but when they nailed Him to the cross, they did not realize they were fulfilling God's will.

> Peter said, *"Him* (Christ), *being delivered by the determinate counsel and foreknowledge of God, ye have taken and by wicked hands have crucified and slain."* Acts 2:23.

But this God of all power was not defeated in this evil act, for the

Lord Jesus was raised from the dead. By it the devil was defeated and all his ministers of (self) righteousness. This is also a great example of Sovereignty and free will operating at the same time.

Judas, the one who betrayed Jesus, had betrayed himself, and met his just due. John wrote, "Jesus knew from the beginning who should betray him. And he said,

> *"no man can come unto me, except it were given unto him of my Father ... Have not I chosen you twelve, and one of you is a devil* (i.e., slanderer) *... He spake of Judas ... for he it was that should betray him, being one of the twelve."* (John 6:64-71.)

Our God cannot fail, lie, or sin. Neither is He frustrated at man's failure.

God is the author of His sovereign grace and mercy.

> *"For he saith to Moses, I will have mercy on whom I will have mercy, and I will have compassion on whom I will have compassion. So it is not of him that willeth, nor of him that runneth, but of God that sheweth mercy... And whom he will, he hardens."* (Rom. 9:15-16, 18.)

Many Christians have doubts about God's sovereignty. Yet there is one aspect of the Christian life where they profess, maybe unknowingly, that God is sovereign. They may say, as many do, "God has done all He can do, now the rest is up to you."

How contradictory! They may stand on their feet and deny this blessed, comforting, enabling doctrine, but when they bend the knees in prayer, asking God to save, do they not realize they are calling on a sovereign God, who only He has the right and the ability to save?

The question is, If God has done all that He can do, why pray to

Him? But we pray knowing He is the only one who can do what man cannot otherwise do. This power belongs to God, and not man. (Excerpts from Sovereign Grace Baptist Proclaimer)

Now that you have a clearer understanding of the Sovereignty of God, let's talk about the Free Will of man.

It's important to see that man is not sovereign. He is rarely in control of the events that shape his life. However, God has still given man a free will to choose his own lifestyle. In effect, we can be evil, nice, straight, gay or be and do anything we want. Our choices, however, comes with consequences.

> *"Be not deceived; God is not mocked: for whatsoever a man soweth, that shall he also reap."* (Gal. 6:7)

Pastor Steve Weaver writes, "A good definition of free will is the ability of the mind to make choices in accordance with our natures."

This definition of "free will" also applies to God's free will. He too is bound by His nature. Therefore, He cannot sin! Why? Because it is not His nature! But God does have a free will and, unlike human beings, He has an accompanying good and holy nature.

Jonathan Edwards, a 17th century Christian preacher and theologian, said that the will is the mind choosing: though there is a distinction between mind and will, the two are inseparable in action. We do not make a choice without our mind's approving that choice. We choose according to our strongest inclination at a given moment.

The Bible teaches that I'm not free to choose God because it is contrary to my nature. That's why we need new natures that are given to us by the Holy Spirit at regeneration.

> *Unless a man is "Born Again" he cannot enter or even see the kingdom of God.* (John 3).

Though man is commanded to seek the Lord while He may be found, and to come to Christ, we watch in vain for man to do so. Romans 3:11 literally reads,

> *"There is no God seeker."*

> John 6:44 says, *"No one can come to Me, (Jesus), unless the Father who sent Me draws him and I will raise him up on the last day."*

Literally, the verse says, "no one is able."

Gerhard Kittel's Theological Dictionary of the New Testament says that the word translated draw in John 6:44 means "to compel by irresistible authority."

It was used in classical Greek for drawing water from a well. We do not entice or persuade water to leave the well; we force it against gravity to come up by drawing it. So it is with us. We are so depraved that God must drag us to himself." (Chosen by God)

The controversy is in whom God has chosen to be His sons and daughters. Hyper-Calvinists believe that some are chosen and some are not from the foundation of the world.

Free Will folks, of which I am one, believe that what Jesus said, as recorded in John 3:16, qualifies all that accept His invitation.

Listen to the verse and pay particular attention to the word, "WHOSOEVER"

> *"For God so loved the world that he gave his only begotten Son, that* **whosoever** *believeth in him should not perish, but have everlasting life."*

Jesus died for the sins of the whole world…every man, woman, boy and girl. The compelling call of God, through Jesus is an open invitation to whosoever will. Theses are the chosen of God that are pulled out of sin and given a new heart that can believe and worship Him.

Now let's look at how free will and sovereignty work hand and hand in our daily lives to fulfill God's master plan for the ages.

Miles Monroe, a famous evangelist, once explained it this way… when God created the earth; He drew up a master plan, like an architect. His master plan took into account every soul and every action that man would take. Nothing was left out.

God is never taken by surprise because He saw it before the world was. It was put into His plan. Then He began to create, taking into account who would accept Jesus and who would not; who would need deliverance; who would need help, etc.

Every prayer and every need was seen beforehand. Your provision was made way back then and is waiting for the time you need it. You just need to receive it by faith.

This pre-design gives us free will to choose without violating God's Sovereignty. I know that some will say, I prayed and believed but didn't get what I asked for. My provision didn't materialize. It could be as James 4:3 says,

> *"Ye ask, and receive not, because ye ask amiss, that ye may consume it upon your lusts."*

David Wilkerson, the author of The Cross & The Switchblade, offers six reasons that prayers go unanswered.

1. Our Prayers Are Aborted… when They Are Not According To God's Will.

2. Our Prayers Can Be Aborted… When They Are Designed To Fulfill An Inner Lust, Dreams, Or Illusions.

3. Our Prayers Can Be Denied… When We Show No Diligence to Assist God In The Answer.

4. Our Prayers Can Be Aborted… By A Secret Grudge Lodged In The Heart Against Another.

5. Our Prayers Can Be Aborted… By Not Expecting Much To Come of Them.

6. Our Prayers Are Aborted… When We Ourselves Attempt To Prescribe How God Should Answer.

The devil's final strategy in deceiving believers is to make them doubt the faithfulness of God in answering prayer.

Satan would have us believe God has shut His ears to our cry and left us to work things out for ourselves. That's just not true. If you do not see the hand of God, you can bet that the problem is with you, not God.

I'd suggest that you go back before the throne of God and stay there until you get an answer. Don't forget to take your Bible with you.

> *"Let us therefore come boldly unto the throne of grace that we may obtain mercy, and find grace to help in time of need."* (Hebrews 4:16)

One final thought. You may not be hearing the Lord because you are not "Born Again." Listen to what Jesus said,

> *"But you do not believe because you are not part of my flock. My sheep hear my voice, and I know them, and they follow me."* John 10:26-27

If you are not hearing His voice, well, what should I say? You may not be of His flock? Only you can determine that. It's a total life-changing commitment to follow Jesus.

Maybe you did not make that kind of commitment. He must be Lord of all or He is not Lord at all.

CLUTTER

Clutter keeps the mind confused,
As images dance through the night.
Lost among those unimportant thoughts,
Are the dreams that once shined so bright.

An endless parade of fear and doubt,
Crowds the mind to destroy our day,
Ever soaring on the wings of the soul,
Until it has formed an evil array.

But clutter is by one's choice,
Of those who listen to its beat.
Better to face imaginations' due
Than to fall into utter defeat.

Be Quiet! Is our spirit's angry cry,
As we call upon the name of the Lord.
Silence is our hearts desired prayer,
Until our minds are again restored.

Written By
John Marinelli

CHAPTER FOURTEEN

Heaven Is A Real Place Believe It or Not

Is there a real heaven? I would say yes because the Bible tells us so. However, the Bible actually speaks of three heavens.

The word Heaven is found seven times in the first chapter of the Bible alone. It is the seventh word into the Bible. In Genesis 1, we see that it means more than the Celestial City.

The First Heaven is spoken of twenty-one times in the Bible. It is where the atmosphere is and where we see blue skies, clouds and birds. The Bible speaks of the birds or fowls of the "air." For example:

Psalm 104:12, "By them shall the fowls of the heaven have their habitation, which sing among the branches."

The "Dew of Heaven" is mentioned nine times.

Another example is found in Genesis 27:28

"Therefore God give thee of the dew of heaven, and the fatness of the earth, and plenty of corn and wine:" The 1st heaven is commonly referred to as the *firmament* which means "expanse or sky." (Genesis 1:8)

The Second Heaven is where the stars and planets are. We would refer to it as "Outer Space." Here are a few scriptures that refer to the 2nd heaven

> *Genesis 1: 14-17, "And God said, Let there be lights in the firmament of the heaven to divide the day from the night; and let them be for signs, and for seasons, and for days, and years: And let them be for lights in the firmament of the heaven to give light upon the earth: and it was so. And God made two great lights; the greater light to rule the day, and the lesser light to rule the night: he made the stars also. And God set them in the firmament of the heaven to give light upon the earth,"* The phrase "stars of heaven" occurs eleven times in scripture.

> *Isaiah 13:10, "For the stars of heaven and the constellations thereof shall not give their light: the sun shall be darkened in his going forth, and the moon shall not cause her light to shine."*

> *Psalm 8:3, 4, "When I consider thy heavens, the work of thy fingers, the moon and the stars, which thou hast ordained; what is man, that thou art mindful of him? and the son of man, that thou visitest him?"*

> *Psalm 19:1, "The heavens declare the glory of God; and the firmament sheweth his handiwork."*

The Third Heaven is the current heaven where God dwells. Although this is a glorious place, this is not the New Heaven described in Revelation 21 and 22. It is far above the sky and our entire known universe. It is a physical place that is full of angels, saints, animals, and much more.

Paul went to the third heaven and came back. (II Corinthians 12:2-4.)

"I knew a man in Christ above fourteen years ago, whether in the body, I cannot tell; or whether out of the body, I cannot tell: God knoweth; such an one caught up to the third heaven. And I knew such a man, whether in the body, or out of the body, I cannot tell: God knows; How that he was caught up into paradise, and heard unspeakable words, which it is not lawful for a man to utter."

Isaiah saw a glimpse of Heaven.

(Isaiah 6:1-7), "In the year that king Uzziah died, I saw also the Lord sitting upon a throne, high and lifted up, and his train filled the temple. Above it stood the seraphims: each one had six wings; with twain he covered his face, and with twain he covered his feet, and with twain he did fly. And one cried unto another, and said, Holy, holy, holy, is the LORD of hosts: the whole earth is full of his glory. And the posts of the door moved at the voice of him that cried, and the house was filled with smoke.

Then said I, Woe is me! for I am undone; because I am a man of unclean lips, and I dwell in the midst of a people of unclean lips: for mine eyes have seen the King, the LORD of hosts. Then flew one of the seraphims unto me, having a live coal in his hand, which he had taken with the tongs from off the altar: And he laid it upon my mouth, and said, Lo, this hath touched thy lips; and thine iniquity is taken away, and thy sin purged."

This text reveals several things about the third heaven:
- The Lord is sitting upon a throne
- The Lord is wearing a robe with a very long train (hem).
- There is a temple in Heaven where He sits.
- Six winged seraphims ceaselessly fly above the throne

of God and cry one to another announcing the holiness of the Lord of Hosts.
- There is an altar of live coals.

John also saw the third heaven and penned the book of Revelation. Here are a few observations:
- There is a door in Heaven (4:1). The door is opened to all who hear the first audible voice and the sound of the trumpet.
- There is a throne set in Heaven. It is the same one Isaiah saw (Isaiah 4:2).
- God who sits on the throne is described as being like jasper (clear crystal) and a sardine stone (dark red). This was the best way John could describe God's glory (4:3).
- There is a rainbow about the throne (4:3). Our rainbows on earth are made of red, orange, yellow, green, blue, indigo, and violet. This one appears as an emerald, which is green. Green represents life.
- Around God's throne are twenty-four seats. There are twenty-four elders, clothed in white raiment, sitting on the seats. They wear crowns of gold (4:4).

For a full list of what the book of Revelation discloses as being in the third heaven, visit **http://www.fbbc.com/messages/kohl_doctrine_ouranology.html** and read Art Kohl's article.

One day these three heavens will no longer exist. (Isaiah 65:17)

"For, behold, I create new heavens and a new earth: and the former shall not be remembered, nor come into mind."

We do not know what the new heavens will look like but we will see a heaven on earth where Jesus is King and we will reign with Him. We shall dwell with Him, on the earth, forever.

John 14:1-4 records Jesus telling His followers that there were many mansions in His Father's house. He even said that He would not have told them if it were not so. I do believe that God has a house/place where He dwells and it is full of redeemed saints, angels and lots more.

If we die before Jesus returns, we will see it and dwell there too until we take that glorious ride on heavenly horseback through time and space with Jesus at His 2nd coming.

I AM THERE

"I AM" There,
At the end of your broken dreams,
Before the sun rises over your day,
Prior to those tear-filled streams.

"I AM" There,
Down that road of despair,
When all seems to be lost,
And no one seems to care.

"I AM" There,
Over all of life's twists and turns,
When tomorrow is all but gone,
And when you are full of concerns.

"I AM" There,
Sayeth the Lord of Host,
To bring you hope and peace,
And the power of my Holy Ghost.

"I AM" There,
To be sure you make it through,
In the midst of every trial,
To bless your life and deliver you.

"I AM" There

Written By
John Marinelli

CHAPTER FIFTEEN

Hell, A Place of Suffering Believe It or Not

Hell is a literal place, just like Heaven. They both play a big part in man's future. For the redeemed; heaven is waiting, for the lost or unsaved, hell is their final destination.

According to Gallup research, 94% of U.S. adults believe in God or a universal spirit; 84% believe Jesus Christ is God or the Son of God; and 53% believe in a literal hell.

A Newsweek poll found that 94% of Americans believe in God; 77% believe in a heaven; 76% think they have a good or excellent chance of getting there. 58% of those surveyed believe in hell.

According to church historian Martin Marty, hell began to disappear from man's thinking in the 19th century, and no one seemed to notice. In rejecting heaven and hell, one also rejects the awesome seriousness of moral and immoral behavior. But for those who take God seriously, human freedom means the capacity to make moral decisions, which have radical and enduring consequences.

In general, more adults in the U.S. believe in hell now than did 40 years ago. The concept was losing ground as recently as 1980 when just over half of those surveyed said they believed in hell. By 1990 the percentage had risen to 60%.

Mathew 7:13-14 records Jesus saying,

> *"Enter ye in at the strait gate: for wide is the gate, and broad is the way, that leads to destruction, and many there be which go in thereat: Because strait is the gate, and narrow is the way, which leads unto life, and few there be that find it."*

There are only two roads in life, one leads to Hell, characterized by destruction and the other road leads to life or heaven. The masses, all the religions that do not accept Jesus as the only way, walk down the broad road. It is wide enough for all to fit. But the road to life is narrow…One Way…Jesus, the Christ of God.

Hell is a reality; a real place for real people. It is so bad that Jesus told the crowd in one of his sermons, (Mathew 18:8-9),

> *"Wherefore if thy hand or thy foot offend thee, cut them off, and cast them from thee: it is better for thee to enter into life halt or maimed, rather than having two hands or two feet to be cast into everlasting fire. And if thine eye offends thee, pluck it out, and cast it from thee: it is better for thee to enter into life with one eye, rather than having two eyes to be cast into hell fire".*

Here are some other references concerning the reality of hell.

Mathew 10:28

> *"And fear not them which kill the body, but are not able to kill the soul: but rather fear him which is able to destroy both soul and body in hell."*

Rev. 20:10

> *"And the devil that deceived them was cast into the lake of fire and brimstone, where the beast and the false prophet*

are, and shall be tormented day and night for ever and ever."

Mathew 25:46

"And these shall go away into everlasting punishment: but the righteous into life eternal." KJV

Mathew 25:41,

"Then shall he say also unto them on the left hand, Depart from me, ye cursed, into everlasting fire, prepared for the devil and his angels:"

In our modern vernacular, hell signifies a place of fire and punishment and this is indeed taught in the scriptures.

Hell is mentioned in the Bible (KJV) 54 times. Hell appears 31 times in the Old Testament and 23 in the New Testament.

In the OT, hell is translated from the Hebrew word "Sheol." In the NT, hell was translated from three words, Tartaroo, Hades and Gehenna. All words express some or all of these characteristics: an eternal separation from God, a place of darkness, suffering, pain and torment. It is not a place where you want to visit or move to.

In my earlier days, we used to say, flippantly, that we'd probably end up in hell, having a party with all our friends. I have since come to my senses, realizing that hell is a place of isolation. Those that go there will suffer all alone forever.

Can you imagine being in total darkness, all alone with just your suffering and pain to keep you company? Don't think that your punishment will be administered by demons or the devil. They will be cast into the lake of fire. There are no jailors to talk to or to call out to…just you, all alone, suffering forever. It's not a pretty picture.

Why would God do this to me?, you might ask… because you rejected the only way to Him, Jesus. He made the way possible by sending Jesus to die for your sins so you could be free to worship Him.

He allowed you to live this long and has constantly called you to Himself in a variety of ways, all with no response. You sidestepped His invitation, ignored His call and refused to accept his destiny for you.

However, God does not send anyone to hell. They chose not to be with Him and Hell is the only other place.

> *"The rich man lifted up his eyes in hell, in torment when he died"* Luke 16:23

And so will you if you reject so great a salvation.

Have I scared you? I hope so because it is no laughing matter. Your eternal destiny is at stake and I want you to know the reality of hell and hopefully keep you from going there…so, here's what you do…

> *" And they said, Believe on the Lord Jesus Christ, and thou shalt be saved"* (Acts 16:31).

FRAGILE FLOWER RED

As a flower in earthen sod,
I bloom for thee, oh God.
To blossom with the turn of spring,
to be to you, a beautiful thing.

I lift my Fragile Flower Red
upward from my earthen bed,
to draw light from God above,
strength and peace and joy and love.

As a flower, I bloom for Thee,
that passersby may stop and see.
Your fragrance and beauty I am,
flowered in grace as a man.

As a flower in earthen sod,
I bloom for Thee, oh God.
Upward, I lift my head,
as a Fragile Flower Red.

Written By John Marinelli

CHAPTER SIXTEEN

The Devil Is Your Enemy Believe It Not

According to the Barna Group, the majority of Christians **do not** believe that Satan or that the devil actually exist. However, according to an AP-AOL news poll, up to 97% of evangelical Christians believe that angels exist.

God is the only eternal self-existent being represented in the Bible (Isaiah 41:4; Isaiah 44:6,8; Isaiah 45:6,21; Revelation 1:8). Satan is not self-existent. Satan must have, therefore, had a point of origin (Romans 11:36; Colossians 1:16; John 1:3; Hebrews 1:2).

God is the Father of all spirits including Satan (Job 12:10; Ephesians 2:2; Hebrews 12:9). He is a created being that rebelled against God.

Satan did not abide in truth (John 8:44). Satan "fell" into condemnation (1 Timothy 3:6).

Angels (demons) were cast into Hades when they sinned (II Peter 2:4). Angels didn't keep their own domain. They abandoned their proper abode and were cast down (Jude 6-7).

War in heaven against Satan's army vs. Michael, the Arc Angel & other angels...Satan was cast "out" of heaven (Revelation 12:7-9).

Satan has already lost his war against God (I Corinthians 15:54-57; Colossians 2:15; Hebrews 2:12-15; Revelation 1:18).

Satan is a defeated foe. Here are a few examples found in the Bible of when he was defeated.

1. War in heaven – cast to earth (Revelation 12:7-9).
2. God "tests" Job with the devil – "you think Job is good, take away blessings…he will curse you" (Job 1:11-12; Job 2:4-6).
3. Temptation in wilderness with Jesus (Matthew 4:1-11).
4. Cast out demons during Jesus'; ministry (Luke 10:17-20).
5. Sinless death & resurrection of Christ (Colossians 2:14-15; Hebrews 2:14-16; 1 John 3:8; Revelation 1:18).
6. Every time a "sinner" becomes a Christian (Acts 26:18: Colossians 1:13), "there is joy in the presence of the angels of God…" (Luke 15:10).

Jesus defeated Satan (otherwise known as, the devil).

"And having spoiled principalities and powers, he made a shew of them openly, triumphing over them in it." (Colossians 2:15).

The idea here is that Jesus bound all of His enemies and paraded around the city dragging them behind, tied to the back of His chariot. It was an "Open Show" for all to see.

I know what you are thinking because I used to think the same thing. If Satan is defeated, having no power, why is he still attacking us?

When the Bible says that Satan is defeated, it means he has no real power of his own but is still loose to attack the saints. Before, he had power and was even called, "the god of this world." (II Corinthians 4:4)

Adam gave that power to him and Jesus took it back. (Mathew 28:18)

"All power" is all power. That leaves none for evil to use except that which you and I give him. Satan can draw power from us but must deceive us into giving it to him.

Eve was a good example of one who was deceived and relinquished her power otherwise known as authority…and Adam followed her example. If we stand on God's Word, we hold on to our authority and cannot be overcome. That's what Jesus did. He said to Satan, "It is written."

> *"Be sober, be vigilant; because your adversary the devil, as a roaring lion, walks about, seeking whom he may devour."* (1Peter 5:8)

I see several things here:

1. He roams the earth…. always looking and checking on us.
2. He is like a roaring lion…it's a scare tactic.
3. He is looking for someone whom he can devour…that means there are many he cannot devour. He looks for those of us that are weak in the faith and are willing to give up on our principles. Remember, the lost are taken at his will because they operate in the flesh and are easily influenced. The believer is whom he, (The devil), is seeking to devour because he does not want us to reveal Christ to the world.
4. We are to be sober, constantly on the lookout for an attack.

We are instructed to steadfastly resist him in the faith…or by faith.

How?, by saying, "it is written" and quoting what is written and believing it with all our hearts.

Example! You are in a bad economy and you lost your job. Satan brings fear to you that everything is going to crash and you will soon be on the street begging for bread. You read the scriptures and see Romans 8:28,

> *"And we know that all things work together for good to them that love God, to them who are the called according to his purpose."*

Who do you believe? the voice in your head or the voice speaking to you from the pages of the Bible?

It's not enough to just hear the Word. You must act upon it for it to be effective. That means you speak it out, over and over until you believe it and Satan is convinced that you will not move off your premise.

If you wavier from what God said, Satan can see it and will keep after you until you fall. Romans 8:28 says in effect, that if I am called according to His purposes and love Him, I can say that He will work *EVERYTHING* together for good. This defeats the attack because it gives me faith and hope to go on and believe God for all my needs. Understand?

So there is a real devil and he roams the earth seeking to devour any believer who is not aware of his tricks and schemes.

Ephesians 6:11 says,

> *"Put on the whole armor of God, that ye may be able to stand against the wiles of the devil."*

Read the chapter and see if you are wearing all the armor. Most Christians don't even know they need armor and some pick and choose which part of the armor they want to wear but never wear it all at one time.

As you review the different parts of God's body armor, realize that all but one, the sword of the Spirit, is defensive.

The sword of the Spirit is the Word of God. That is offensive to the pulling down of accusations, lies, tormenting spirits, fear and all the other stuff Satan can throw at you. It has two edges and can cut deep every time.

Jesus compared Himself to Satan as opposites (John 10:10a). He said,

> *"The thief cometh not, but for to steal, and to kill, and to destroy: I am come that they might have life, and that they might have it more abundantly."*

Satan will try to steal your peace, hope and everything else that you do not give to the Lord. Jesus, on the other hand, will give you a life that is full of abundance…Love, peace, love, longsuffering and all the rest of the fruits of His Spirit.

John 10:10b should not be used as though it gives some promise of an improved physical life for the Christian. Such a view, in light of the context of the chapter, is shallow, and it overlooks the profound truth of the passage.

The passage promises superior, superabundant spiritual life, life empowered by the indwelling of Jesus Christ. This is what Paul meant when he said he counted all things loss that he might win Christ.

John 10:10 is a promise of spiritual dimension to life, not physical abundance. A focus on the physical trivializes the profound depth of John 10:10. That's why I tied abundance, in the previous paragraph, with the fruit of the Spirit.

Some preachers use John 10:10b to support an abundance of stuff, saying that is why Jesus came…so we could get out of debt and live as a rich person. Their focus is on materialism instead of Spiritual Fruit. Jesus also said, as Mathew recorded in 6:33,

> *"But seek ye first the kingdom of God, and his righteousness; and all these things shall be added unto you."*

The emphasis has never been on seeking material things. Jesus clearly says man's first priority is the Lord and His righteousness. Things will be given to us because we need them to live and do His will.

Wealth, i.e. the abundance of things, is relative to the society we live in. In some countries, families with a tin roof instead of a thatch style roof are considered wealthy.

It is true that God gives us the power to gain wealth.

> *"But thou shalt remember the LORD thy God: for it is he that giveth thee power to get wealth, that he may establish his covenant which he sware unto thy fathers, as it is this day."* (Deuteronomy 8:18)

However, the wealth gained is to be used to establish the covenant between you and the Lord.

It's time to declare victory over Sin, Satan, Death, Worry, Fear, All Demons, and Anything Else that keeps you from experiencing the love of God.

QUIET HOURS

In the silence of the quiet hours,
In the presence of a new dawn,
I bow down upon my knees,
For bringing me life reborn.

Taking off all the shackles,
Letting my spirit free.
I give all the thanks to Jesus,
For giving His love to me.

Written By
Marilyn Marinelli

CHAPTER SEVENTEEN

The Rapture of The Church Believe It or Not

Here's a truth that has been hidden in plan sight for centuries. The rapture of the church is a point of contention among Christian groups. I personally believe that Jesus will return for His church and it will be a quick departure from this earth.

It's been said that Jesus will come for His church on earth and rapture or take it up quickly into His presence. It is a catching away of all Christians, real ones, not religious, fake or even churchgoers that play church for other selfish reasons.

The word *rapture* (in Greek *harpazo*, in Latin *rapere*) means to be caught up or taken away suddenly. The rapture refers to the sudden removal of all of God's people on the earth.

In the twinkling of an eye, "Born Again" Christians will suddenly be transformed out of their human bodies and will rise up into the air to join Jesus Christ.

There is a reason Christ warned his followers 13 times in the New Testament to not be deceived, and to watch and be ready. He wanted us to be excited about His glorious appearing.

Satan, on the other hand, does not want us to be excited. He is the master deceiver; the father of lies and wants us to believe his deception rather than the signs of Christ's return given to us by Jesus himself. The devil will send many lies to deceive us and to rob us of the joy of living every day in anticipation of Christ's return.

For those who believe that the Bible is the truth and is the very Word of God, it's easy to believe in and rejoice in the prophecies that tell of the rapture of God's church.

The Bible tells us of others who have been taken up into heaven in very much the same way that we will be at the time of our departure.

Elijah was taken up into heaven like a whirlwind. I Kings 2:11-12

> *"As they were walking along and talking together, suddenly a chariot of fire and horses of fire appeared and separated the two of them, and Elijah went up to heaven in a whirlwind. Elisha saw this and cried out, "My father! My father! The chariots and horsemen of Israel! And Elisha saw him no more."*

Enoch was also taken from this life so that he would not experience death. Hebrews 11:5

> *"By faith Enoch was taken from this life, so that he did not experience death; he could not be found, because God had taken him away. For before he was taken, he was commended as one who pleased God, and without faith it is impossible to please God, because anyone who comes to him must believe that he exists and that he rewards those who earnestly seek him."*

So, when will the church be raptured? We know there is more evidence today that He is coming for His Church soon, than at any other time in history.

As these signs intensify, all of us who know Christ as our savior will be looking toward heaven and awaiting for the coming of our Lord.

Many biblical scholars feel that the rapture will occur prior to the "Tribulation Period", or a pre-tribulation rapture. Thus God will spare His church from the persecutions of the Antichrist and the wrath of God that will fall upon the inhabitants of the earth during the end times.

Those who come to Christ following the rapture will live through the persecution of Christians by the Antichrist. Some will face martyrdom for their faith.

There are several other views of the timing for the rapture of the church; however, here we will examine the pre-tribulation view and the biblical support for it.

One of the best supporting verses from the Bible for the rapture of the church is found in Revelation 3:10.

> *"Because you have kept my command to persevere, I also will keep you from the hour of trial which shall come upon the whole world to test those who dwell on the earth."*

I would assume that God would not bring the same type of judgment to His children, as He will on the wicked. This scripture seems to support my premise. The assumption is that believers will be taken out of harms way.

Listen to what Paul tells the Thessalonians in his second letter, chapter two verses 2-15.

> *"Now we beseech you, brethren, by the coming of our Lord Jesus Christ, and by our gathering together unto him,*
>
> *[2] That ye be not soon shaken in mind, or be troubled, neither by spirit, nor by word, nor by letter as from us, as that the day of Christ is at hand.*

³ *Let no man deceive you by any means: for that day shall not come, except there come a falling away first, and that man of sin be revealed, the son of perdition;*

⁴ *Who opposes and exalts himself above all that is called God, or that is worshipped; so that he, as God, sitts in the temple of God, shewing himself that he is God.*

⁵ *Remember ye not, that, when I was yet with you, I told you these things?*

⁶ *And now ye know what withholds that he might be revealed in his time.*

⁷ *For the mystery of iniquity doth already work:* **only he who now letteth will let,** *(Restrain),* **until he be taken out of the way.**

⁸ *And then shall that wicked be revealed, whom the Lord shall consume with the spirit of his mouth, and shall destroy with the brightness of his coming:*

⁹ *Even him, whose coming is after the working of Satan with all power and signs and lying wonders,*

¹⁰ *And with all deceivableness of unrighteousness in them that perish; because they received not the love of the truth that they might be saved.*

¹¹ *And for this cause God shall send them strong delusion, that they should believe a lie:*

¹² *That they all might be damned who believed not the truth, but had pleasure in unrighteousness.*

[13] But we are bound to give thanks always to God for you, brethren beloved of the Lord, because God hath from the beginning chosen you to salvation through sanctification of the Spirit and belief of the truth:

[14] Whereunto he called you by our gospel, to the obtaining of the glory of our Lord Jesus Christ.

[15] Therefore, brethren, stand fast, and hold the traditions, which ye have been taught, whether by word, or our epistle.

I wanted to show the context so there is no misunderstanding. Note verse seven…he that letteth is God's Holy Spirit. He is a restraining force in the world, holding evil back from its ultimate expression.

When the Spirit is taken out of the way, guess what? the Spirit is in us and Jesus said He would never leave us comfortless but will be with us until the end of the age. (John 14:18)

When that moment has come and it is the end of the age, we will go with the Spirit to meet Jesus in the air as Paul says in 1 Thessalonians 4:17.

There you have it. The rapture or sudden removal of God's children is at hand. The big question now is will you be left behind?

Non-believers will be left to face the great tribulation where God pours out His wrath upon the wicked. You don't want to be in that group of folks.

IN THE TWINKLE OF AN EYE

In the twinkle of an eye,
The Lord will come for me.
Before you can even blink,
I'll be with Jesus in eternity.

In the twinkle of an eye,
The trump of God will sound,
And all who love the Lord
Will be homeward bound.

In the twinkle of an eye,
The World will fall into despair.
When God's wrath is poured out,
Upon all who do not care.

In the twinkle of an eye,
We shall shout the victory.
Spared from His judgment,
To complete our divine destiny.

Written By John Marinelli

CHAPTER EIGHTEEN

Final Judgment Believe It or Not

The Bible clearly states that Judgment will follow death.

> *"And as it is appointed unto men once to die, but after this the judgment:"* (Hebrews 9:27)

We all will die some day and according to this scripture, we all will face judgment. The time and date is out there somewhere in the future, closer for some of us than for others.

It's interesting to learn that death is an appointment. I bet you never knew you had an appointment with death. That's one appointment that we wish we could break.

There are different judgments. We will not all be summoned to the same court. By the way, these judgments have no court of appeal. The Bible talks about two judgments, one for the lost or unsaved and one for the saved.

The believer will appear before the Judgment Seat of Christ.

> *"For we must all appear before the judgment seat of Christ; that every one may receive the things done in his body, according to that he hath done, whether it be good or bad."* (II Corinthians 5:10)

The resurrected saints will receive rewards for the good works they performed while on earth.

Remember, *"There is therefore now no condemnation to them which are in Christ Jesus, who walk not after the flesh, but after the Spirit."* (Romans 8:1).

The application of "no condemnation" is exclusive to those **who walk after the Spirit**.

The Christian that walks in the flesh will also appear at the Judgment Seat of Christ. They will experience loss but will not lose his or her salvation.

It's all about rewards. Paul pictures Christ seated on a magistrate's judgment seat, The Bema, as though He were a judge of an athletic competition, a place where rewards were given out and losses clearly seen by all in attendance.

In other words, it is a reward seat and portrays a time of rewards or loss of rewards following examination, but it is not a time of punishment where believers are judged for their sins. Such would be inconsistent with the finished work of Christ on the Cross-, because He totally paid the penalty for our sins.

This event will occur immediately following the rapture or resurrection of the church after it is caught up to be with the Lord in the air as described in 1 Thessalonians 4:13-18. **J. Hampton Keathley III**, of www.Bible.org, offers three great scriptures in support of rewards instead of judgment.

1. In Luke 14:12-14, reward is associated with the resurrection and the rapture is when the church is resurrected.

2. In Revelation 19:8, when the Lord returns with His bride at the end of the tribulation, she is seen already rewarded. Her reward is described as fine linen; the righteous acts of the saints—undoubtedly the result of rewards.

3. In 2nd Timothy 4:8 and 1 Corinthians 4:5, rewards are associated with "that day" and with the Lord's coming. Again, for the church this means the event of 1 Thessalonians 4:13-18.

He further states…So the order of events will be:

A. the rapture which includes our glorification or resurrection bodies,

B. exaltation into the heavens with the Lord,

C. examination before the *Bema*, and (d) compensation or rewards.

The Purpose of the Bema

(1) To evaluate the quality of every believer's work whether it is good or bad, i.e., acceptable and thus worthy of rewards, or unacceptable, to be rejected and unworthy of rewards. Actually an evaluation is going on every day by the Lord (Rev. 2-3).

(2) To destroy and remove unacceptable production portrayed in the symbols of wood, hay, and stubble. All sinful deeds, thoughts, and motives, as well as all good deeds done in the energy of the flesh will be consumed like wood, hay, and stubble before a fire because they are unworthy of reward. Why? This will be answered as we consider the basis on which rewards are given or lost.

(3) To reward the believer for all the good he or she has done as portrayed by the symbols of gold, silver, and precious stones, that which is valuable and can stand the test of fire without being consumed.

I see it as an examination of how well we abide in Christ while here on earth. How well did we walk in the Spirit, revealing God's love and grace to others? Did our lights shine or did they dim and eventually burn out?

Theologians tell us that the "Bema Seat" experience will happen immediately after the rapture. I think it will be a glorious time of fellowship with other believers and great joy to be in the presence of our Lord.

Yes, there will be loss of rewards because they were not motivated by the Spirit but rather done in the flesh. Wood, Hay & Stubble that will burn away, characterizes the deeds done in the flesh.

The final Judgment will be the "Great White Throne Judgment." It is reserved for all people who have rejected God's call to salvation. Every person who has lived upon planet earth and has refused to accept God's way of redemption will face their creator and be judged.

Many that thought they were safe will be shocked. Jesus, as recorded in Mathew 7:23 will say to them,

> *"And then will I profess unto them, I never knew you: depart from me, ye that work iniquity."*

I believe these to be all the religions of the world. But also, many who were called Christian but were members of a church and not truly "Born Again." Verses 21 & 22 tell the story.

> *"Not every one that saith unto me, Lord, Lord, shall enter into the kingdom of heaven; but he that doeth the will of my Father, which is in heaven. ^{22} Many will say to me in that day, Lord, Lord, have we not prophesied in thy name? and in thy name have cast out devils? and in thy name done many wonderful works?"*

This is religion without the guidance and control of the Holy Spirit. These are also they that will go through the tribulation and still not be saved.

The concept of a great white throne comes from Revelation 20:11-15,

> *"And I saw a great white throne, and him that sat on it, from whose face the earth and the heaven fled away; and there was found no place for them. And I saw the dead, small and great, stand before God; and the books were opened: and another book was opened, which is the book of life: and the dead were judged out of those things which were written in the books, according to their works.*
>
> *And the sea gave up the dead, which were in it; and death and hell delivered up the dead, which were in them: and they were judged every man according to their works. And death and hell were cast into the lake of fire. This is the second death. And whosoever was not found written in the book of life was cast into the lake of fire".*

Note that there is a, *"Book of Life"* filled with the names of the redeemed. If your name is not there, you can put it there now, before it's too late by asking Jesus to save your soul and committing yourself to Him.

Another point is that the dead, both great & small are all there. That's the famous and the nobodies. The text seems to suggest that all mankind including the redeemed are there but it is important to see that the verse says, "The Dead". All the folks that are living are listed in the Book of Life and are enjoying eternal bliss.

I know what you are going to say, "Why then is the Book of Life" at this judgment? I believe it is there as a final condemnation. It's to prove that they did not receive God's plan of salvation.

Guess who is sitting on this great white throne?

> *"For the Father judgeth no man, but hath committed all judgment unto the Son: That all men should honour the Son, even as they honour the Father. He that honoureth not the Son honoureth not the Father which hath sent him".* (John 5:22-23)

> *"In the day when God shall judge the secrets of men by Jesus Christ according to my gospel."* (Romans 2:16)

You guessed it. It is none other than Jesus. He would know if your name is in His book, right?

The greatness of this throne is not in the size of it, nor is it the number of the multitude who stands convicted before it, but in the greatness of the Judge who presides over it--the Lord Jesus.

The white color is representative of His holiness and purity, and of how fitting it is that He should judge mankind.

> **"But they that wait upon the LORD shall renew their strength; they shall mount up with wings as eagles; they shall run, and not be weary; and they shall walk, and not faint."** Isaiah 40:31

CHAPTER NINETEEN

The End of The World Believe It or Not

Remember the scare that took place from a prophecy about the coming of our Lord? The end of the world is near, they said—December 21, 2012, to be exact. However, that date has come and gone and we are still here.

According to theories based on a purported ancient **Maya** prediction and fanned by the marketing machine behind the **2012 movie**, life on earth was supposed to end.

But what does the Bible have to say about the end of planet earth? Noel Horner's article in The Good News says this about that.

Nearly two millennia ago the disciples of Jesus of Nazareth asked Him a question that has intrigued people ever since:

"What shall be the sign of thy coming, and of the end of the world?" (Mathew 24:3).

People in every generation since have wondered about this. Will the world literally end? If so, how? Why? And when? What does the Bible really say about this crucial and disturbing question?

Here are a few signs of the times that Jesus told His disciples; there would be many wars and other conflicts between nations and ethnic groups. He also spoke of famines, massive disease epidemics and earthquakes.

Robin Calamaio, in her article, The End of The World And The Bible, says, the heavens and earth will be melted down and recreated (II Pet 3:7-13). The new heavens and earth will be eternal and very different from our current order. There will be no decay (Romans 8:19-22) and no longer any curse (Gen 3:17-19 and Rev 22:3).

There will be no need for the sun or the moon's light (Rev 21:23) and yet, there will be no nighttime (Rev21:1,25).

Death will no longer exist. Mourning, crying and pain will pass away (Rev 21:4). All animals will peacefully coexist (Isaiah 11:6-9). Only righteousness will exist (II Pet 3:13 and Rev 21:8,27) with Jesus visibly ruling this active eternal state (Rev 22:5). The coming marvels are incomprehensible (Rev 21:24 and I Cor 2:9).

Many of the references related to the end of the world, actually mean the end of the age.

The age that will end is where Satan, sin and materialism rule. The actual earth will be cleansed and refitted as a new earth for habitation by Jesus and His saints. I guess we can look for better days ahead.

> Jesus said, "*No one knows about that day or hour, not even the angels in heaven, nor the Son, but only the Father. As it was in the days of Noah, so it will be at the coming of the Son of Man. For in the days before the flood, people were eating and drinking, marrying and giving in marriage, up to the day Noah entered the ark; and they knew nothing about what would happen until the flood came and took them all away.*"

That is how it will be at the coming of the Son of Man.

*"Two men will be in the field; one will be taken and the other left. Two women will be grinding with a hand mill; one will be taken and the other left. **Therefore, keep watch**, because you do not know on what day your Lord will come."*(Mathew 24:36-42) NIV

Why doesn't God show up now and end all this? C.S. Lewis, a novelist, poet, academic, medievalist, literary critic, essayist, lay theologian and Christian apologist from Belfast, Ireland, (1898-1963), gives this answer.

"God will invade. But I wonder whether people who ask God to interfere openly and directly in our world quite realize what it will be like when He does. When that happens, it is the end of the world. When the author walks on to the stage, the play is over.

God is going to invade, all right, but what is the good of saying you are on His side, when you see the whole natural universe melting away like a dream and something else--something it never entered your head to conceive--comes crashing in; something so beautiful to some of us and so terrible to others, (The lost), that none of us will have any choices left?

For this time it will be God without disguise; something so overwhelming that it will strike either irresistible love or irresistible horror into every creature.

It will be too late then to choose your side... That will not be the time for choosing: it will be the time when we discover which side we really have chosen, whether we realized it before or not.

Now, today, this moment is our chance to choose the right side. God is holding back to give us that chance. It will not last forever. We must take it or leave it. We must Believe It or Not. The truth is before us, hidden in plain sight.

The Bible gives many examples of signs that should warn us of the coming end of the age. Jesus gives six such signs, Paul gives two characteristics, and eleven other occurrences are given by the prophets to occur prior to or soon after the end of the age.

While we are also told we will not know the time of the End, God obviously wanted us to know when that time was getting closer.

As the Christian church is increasingly drawn into the interfaith movement, and as more and more churches go into isolation, preparing to sleep through the growing attacks on their faith, perhaps God knew it would take a few signs to wake us up and remind us that we have work to do.

It is increasingly obvious that the time of our Lord's coming is drawing near. Prophecy is being fulfilled daily, and at a faster pace than ever before. Whether you believe in a pre-tribulation rapture, or believe Christians will be witness to the full tribulation, wrath, and final judgments, matters not.

The beginning of birth pains and the signs of the times should have the same effect on all of us. It should motivate us to save as many souls as we can in the time that we have left. The Great Commission tells us to be disciples to all nations, bringing the message of salvation through Christ to all people.

If the Church is raptured before the tribulation, it is important that we leave behind an explanation for the trials and judgments those left behind will face. How else will they recognize the deception of the anti-Christ and seek instead the truth of the Bible?

If you believe that we are to endure the tribulation along side them, you will need to be prepared to not only share the message of salvation, but share with them the reasons for God's judgment and hold it up as further proof of their need to be saved.

Here's what to look for to know we are in the end times and the end of the age is near.

1. **Matthew 24:11** *"And many false prophets will arise, and will mislead many."*

2. **Matthew 24:6** *"And you will be hearing of wars and rumors of wars; see that you are not frightened, for those things must take place, but that is not yet the end."*

3. **Matthew 24:7** *"For nation will rise against nation, and kingdom against kingdom, and in various places there will be famines and earthquakes."*

4. **Matthew 24:8-9** *"But all these things are merely the beginning of birth pangs. Then shall they deliver you up to be afflicted, and shall kill you: and ye shall be hated of all nations for my name's sake."*

5. **Matthew 24:14** *"And this gospel of the kingdom shall be preached in the whole world for a witness to all the nations, and then the end shall come."*

6. **II Timothy 3:1-5,7** *"But realize this, that in the last days difficult times will come. For men will be lovers of self, lovers of money, boastful, arrogant, disobedient to their parents, ungrateful, unholy, unloving, unforgiving, malicious gossips, without self-control, brutal, haters of good, treacherous, reckless, conceited, lovers of pleasure rather than lovers of god; holding to a form of godliness, although they have denied its power; always learning and never able to come to the knowledge of the truth."*

7. **I Timothy 4:1-3** *" Now the Spirit speaketh expressly, that in the latter times some shall depart from the faith, giving heed to seducing spirits, and doctrines of devils; Speaking lies in hypocrisy; having their conscience seared with a hot iron; Forbidding to marry, and commanding to abstain from meats, which God hath created to be received with thanksgiving of them which believe and know the truth.."*

The Apostle John, author of the book of Revelation, prophesied of seven deadly sins that were prevalent among those living in the, "End Times." (Rev. 9:13-21) These sins are; **demon worship, idolatry, murder, magic/witchcraft, sexual immorality, theft,** and **refusal to repent**. Rev. 9:13-21

This is a portrait of the period of time during the tribulation but it is important to know that most of the seven deadly sins are present today in our society.

Luke gives us the record of what Jesus said to do when we see these things, (Luke 21:28),

> *"But when these things begin to take place, straighten up and lift up your heads, because your redemption is drawing near."*

CHAPTER TWENTY

Spiritual Warfare Believe It or Not

We already know, from previous chapters, that we indeed have a real enemy that roams the earth looking for someone to devour. (1 Peter 5:8) We also know that God has made armor for us to wear so we can stand against the wilds of the devil. (Eph. 6:11)

What most Christians don't know is that there is a war, that they are expected to fight the enemies of God, and how to identify those that seek their harm. Why fight?, because we are under attack.

Paul tells the Ephesian believers, chapter 6:12,

> *"For we wrestle not against flesh and blood, but against principalities, against powers, against the rulers of the darkness of this world, against spiritual wickedness in high places."*

It is critical to know that our battle is not with flesh and blood.

That takes into account family, friends, co-workers, folks that do not like you, those who have betrayed or hurt you, those who have slandered your name and good character and everyone else with a bad attitude.

We are not in a battle with people. However, we are in a battle with unseen powers of evil that use people against us. The people are just thorns in our flesh. God's grace should be sufficient.

I always thought that I could not assert myself against folks that were mean to me because of Ephesians 6:12. I just took the blow and tried to forgive…until I realized that the devil was behind it all, coming through certain folks to destroy my confidence, and self-respect.

The Bible tells us that Satan is the accuser of the brethren. (I Timothy 4:13) He uses arrogant puffed-up people to sling accusations and attitudes against us so we will agree with him and fall from our faith.

In reality, we are instructed in I Peter 5:8-9 to *resist the devil steadfastly in the faith.*

Here's what that means to me.

1. We can and should respond to the attacker's lies with what is true, even if that person will not listen. By standing up, we are listening to what we are saying and it will strengthen our faith by doing so.

2. When we resist, *"In The Faith"*, we are standing on the Word of God demonstrating our resolve that; we have been forgiven; that the past sins no longer exist; that we are under the Lordship of Christ and…

"we know that all things work together for good to them that love God, to them who are the called according to his purpose." (Romans 8:28)

3. Our primary focus is to do the will of God. Other things just do not count. Jesus told one who wanted to bury his father before he could follow Him. Here's what Jesus told that man,

> *"Jesus said unto him, let the dead bury their dead: but you go and preach the kingdom of God."* (Luke 9:59-60)

We must know our enemy. We must also know the scriptures and ourselves to be victorious in spiritual warfare.

Knowing the enemy is to acknowledge that he exists and that he is here with one single purpose in mind, to steal, and to kill, and to destroy (John 10:10) We have already established that his power and authority was stripped from him when Jesus died on the cross. He is a defeated foe. (Colossians 2:15).

However, he is a master at deception. He must get you to agree with his lie. This gives him power over you. With it, he suggests actions that will lead you to destruction…things like; it's ok to have sex outside of marriage, abortion is the right thing to do, homosexuality is just an alternate lifestyle and not a sin, smoking will not kill you, drugs are cool, and so on.

If you fall for the lie, you end up participating in it, even if it's just in your mind. The end result is the pollution of your soul and the destruction of your spiritual walk with God.

Knowing yourself is also half the battle because most of the lies that fall from Satan's bag of tricks are about you…all the things you've done wrong and the way you were 10 or 20 years ago. He will constantly bring past sins up, even if God forgave you, until you believe that you are still the same guy or gal as back then.

A reformed prostitute, who is now a wife and mother, saved by the blood of Jesus, will often, face her past many times. If she does not know that God has washed away her sins, she will stay in regret, guilt and depression.

However, if she holds on to the "New Creature" teachings of Paul, the apostle in Romans chapter 12, she can easily say, *"that is no longer me."*

> *"I am a new creature in Christ and do not have to go back or even look back. My purpose now is to soar like the eagle above the clouds of despair and accusations of evil spirits."*

The victory is so great that her new life is like a butterfly that came out of a transformation from a caterpillar. They are just not the same creatures anymore.

Knowing the Word of God seals your victory and is how you walk in the Spirit.

Applying the truths found in the Bible causes you to walk in them. They are not only Spiritual but alive with power to raise you up from being the tail to being the head.

> *"And the LORD shall make thee the head, and not the tail; and thou shalt be above only, and thou shalt not be beneath; if that thou hearken unto the commandments of the LORD thy God, which I command thee this day, to observe and to do them"* (Deuteronomy 28:13).

It is our responsibility to know the truth and to walk in it. Colossians 2:10 says,

> *"And you have been given fullness in Christ who is head over every power and authority".*

He is the head and wants us to rule with Him in this life as well as the one to come. We must see ourselves as He sees us, redeemed, blessed, and righteous in Him."

The Lord showed me an acrostic that helped me to remember the offensive weapons available and how to use them to keep me free. Here they are.

1. **K-The Knowledge of God**, *"Casting down imaginations, and every high thing that exalteth itself against the knowl-*

edge of God, and bringing into captivity every thought to the obedience of Christ" (II Corinthians 10:5)

We are to cast down imaginations and we could have many from sexual to being rich and powerful to almost anything. These thoughts are to be brought captive by obeying Christ and His word.

2. **N-Name of Jesus**. *"That at the name of Jesus every knee should bow, of things in heaven, and things in earth, and things under the earth"* (Philippians 2:10).

It is important to know that every knee, meaning everyone or thing, must yield to the Name of Jesus. In the name of Jesus, demons must flee.

3. **O-Obedience of Christ**, (II Cor.10:5) We must be obedient to the call and will of God.

Rebellion does not sit well with the exercise of victory. Christ's obedience was exact and fulfilled the Law of God perfectly. If we are obedient, we will bring every thought into the subjection of His righteousness. This action will destroy the evil thought before it takes hold in our minds.

4. **B-Blood of Christ**, *"But with the precious blood of Christ, as of a lamb without blemish and without spot"* (I Peter 1:19).

Jesus was God's spotless lamb, a portrait of all the sacrifices from times past that were a foreshadow of Him. He was the ultimate sacrifice. His blood forever paid the price for our sin. I John 1:9 says,

"If we confess our sins, he is faithful and just to forgive us our sins, and to cleanse us from all unrighteousness."

Knowing we are forgiven keeps us free from Satan's attacks that dwell on past sins. We can boldly declare that the blood of Christ continually cleanses us, stopping any attack.

5. **S-Sword of The Spirit**, *"Take the sword of the Spirit, which is the word of God."*(Ephesians 6:17.)

The Word of God is the Bible. There are over 3,000 promises and lots of wisdom, knowledge and help to meet all your needs. Use it.

Charles Spurgeon, a famous minister in the late 1800's and early 1900's, said this about spiritual warfare and Christians.

(Spurgeon was called the Prince of Preachers. He had the very first mega church in England)

Spurgeon said that to be a Christian is to be a warrior. He went on to say:

> "The good soldier of Jesus Christ must not expect to find ease in this world: it is a battlefield. Neither must he reckon upon the friendship of the world; for that would be enmity against God. His occupation is war. As he puts on piece by piece of the panoply provided for him, he may wisely say to himself, this warns me of danger; this prepares me for warfare."

> "Many try compromise; but if you are a true Christian, you can never do compromise.

> The language of deceit fits not a holy tongue. The adversary is the father of lies, and those that are with him understand the art of equivocation; but saints abhor it. If we discuss terms of peace, and attempt to gain something by policy, we have entered upon a course from which we shall return in disgrace."

> "We have no order from the Captain of our salvation to

patch up a truce, and get as good a settlement as we can. We are not sent out to offer concessions.

It is said that if we yield a little, perhaps the world will yield a little also, and good may come of it. If we are not too strict and narrow, perhaps sin will kindly consent to be more decency. Our association with it will prevent its being so barefaced and atrocious.

If we are not narrow-minded, our broad doctrine will go down with the world, and those on the other side will not be so greedy of error as they now are. No such thing. It Ain't going to happen.

Neither may we hope to gain by being neutral, or granting an occasional truce. We are not to cease from conflict, and try to be as agreeable as we can with our Lord's foes, frequenting their assemblies, and tasting their dainties. No such orders are written here. You are to grasp your weapon, and go forth to fight."

CHAPTER TWENTY-ONE

Salvation By Grace Believe It or Not

Here's another truth that is hidden in plain sight, Salvation by grace. It is so misunderstood that it's not funny.

> *"For by grace are ye saved through faith; and that not of yourselves: it is the gift of God"* (Ephesians 2:8.)

This scripture seems to leave out any kind of works of righteousness as part of man's salvation yet many Christian groups adhere to works as well as grace.

Man's salvation is just that, a gift of God. It comes to us through faith, not works. If I have faith in the finished work of Christ, I am saved.

> *"Not of works, lest any man should boast."* (Ephesians 2:9)

Paul, the author of the Ephesian letter, makes it clear that works will not save you and is not necessary as a qualifier for salvation. Maybe he got this idea of, "Grace Only", from Jesus. John's gospel records Jesus saying these words,

> *"For God so loved the world, that he gave his only begotten Son, that whosoever believeth in him should not perish, but have everlasting life."* (John 3:16)

Believing in the Son of God is the qualifier to be saved, so Jesus says. He also says that the Son was sent or given as an act of God, who so loved us that He gave. When you add works to this equation, you change the foundation and make man's eternal destiny subject to his or her deeds and not the Blood of Christ.

We were hopelessly lost and dead in our sins when Christ died for us.

> *"But God demonstrates his own love for us in this; while we were still sinners, Christ died for us."* (Romans 5:8 NIV)

> *"Even when we were dead in sins, hath quickened us together with Christ, (by grace ye are saved;)".* (Ephesians 2:5)

> *"And you, being dead in your sins and the uncircumcision of your flesh, hath he quickened together with him, having forgiven you all trespasses."* (Colossians 2:13)

Paul tells the Roman, Ephesians, and Colossian believers that they were dead in sin when Christ died as the sacrifice for sin; that God quickened them together with Christ, which means; **made alive** with Him; and even has forgiven ALL trespasses. He never added man's works. In fact, he said that it was by grace that they were saved.

If man could work his way to heaven, he'd have to obey the Laws of God perfectly. If he were to falter, even on one small point, he would be a sinner and guilty before a holy and righteous God.

> (Ezekiel 18:20-***The soul*** **who *sins shall die*)** *NIV.*

Why then does the church, for centuries, argue over grace or works? I believe that Christians who add works feel that grace is just too good to be true.

Why would God give us so great a gift with no strings attached? Grace is actually, un-merited favor. That means you do not deserve it…that you did nothing worthy enough to merit it, yet God favored you with it anyway.

The only reason God would do such a thing is because He sent His Only Begotten Son as a sacrifice for sin and condemned sin in the flesh, His righteous flesh, on the cross.

Jesus paid the penalty for sin, which was death. God can now give us this great gift of salvation by Grace through which we can access His love and affection and enjoy Him as He originally intended.

When God looks at us, He sees Jesus. Why? Because we are "Born Again."

> *"and have put on the new man, (Jesus), that is created after God in righteousness and true holiness."*

We are in Him and our sins are washed away forever. (I Corinthians 1:30)

If Satan can get you to believe in works for salvation, you will begin to operate in the flesh. Your belief in Grace will diminish and that's just what is happening today.

Some churches even claim that Jesus' death for sin was only for our past sins and all from the point of salvation forward must be confessed or our salvation is lost.

The problem with that is we are not aware of most of our sin. It is built into our nature and we do it without thinking. No person could catch every sin to confess it.

We would be constantly confessing sins and hoping we didn't miss any. Our ultimate salvation ends up resting in how well we perform and not on the Finished Work of Christ.

He died once for all sin. So, how does works fit into anything? It doesn't.

Do we sit back then and do nothing because we are saved? God forbid! The church has confused faith and salvation for centuries. Listen to what James says about faith and works.

The apostle James said,

> *"Yea, a man may say, Thou hast faith, and I have works: shew me thy faith without thy works, and I will shew thee my faith by my works."*

It's important to see that James is not talking about salvation. He is talking about faith. The evidence of faith is found in the actions of the believer.

On the other hand, the evidence of salvation is seen in whom the believer puts his or her trust.

James said he would show his faith, not salvation, by his actions. If you are not involved in the work of your Heavenly Father, you do not need faith. However, you should be involved. It is God's Will.

DON'T WORRY
(Matthew 6:34)

Don't worry about tomorrow.
You did that yesterday.
Go on with your life,
And remember always to pray.

Ask and it shall be given to you,
But this great truth you already know.
REJOYCE AND BE HAPPY, Why?
Your harvest comes from what you sow.

I will say it again and even more,
Until it becomes crystal clear.
Tomorrow will take care of itself,
But worry is another word for fear.

Now here's what I want you to do.
Trust in the Lord and be of good cheer.
Drop the worry from your vocabulary
And cast out that demon of fear.

Written By
John Marinelli

CHAPTER TWENTY-TWO

The Gifts of The Spirit Are For Today Believe It or Not

Are the gifts of the Holy Spirit available for use by today's believer? Or did they cease with the death of the apostles? This is another source of friction in the 21st century church. I personally believe that the gifts are for today and are in operation even as we live and breathe.

I want to separate Spiritual gifts from Spiritual fruit because they are very different. (Galatians 5:22) offer a list but they should be looked at as "Fruit." It is the fruit of the Spirit.

The gifts of the Holy Spirit are listed in I Corinthians chapter twelve.

> *"Now concerning spiritual gifts, brethren, I would not have you ignorant. Ye know that ye were Gentiles, carried away unto these dumb idols, even as ye were led.* ^{3} *Wherefore I give you to understand, that no man speaking by the Spirit of God calleth Jesus accursed: and that no man can say that Jesus is the Lord, but by the Holy Ghost."* (I Cor. 12:1)

> *"Now there are diversities of gifts, but the same Spirit.* ^{5} *And there are differences of administrations, but the same Lord.*

⁶ And there are diversities of operations, but it is the same God, which worketh all in all.

⁷ But the manifestation of the Spirit is given to every man to profit withal.

⁸ For to one is given by the Spirit the word of wisdom; to another the word of knowledge by the same Spirit; ⁹ To another faith by the same Spirit; to another the gifts of healing by the same Spirit; ¹⁰ To another the working of miracles; to another prophecy; to another discerning of spirits; to another divers kinds of tongues; to another the interpretation of tongues:

¹¹ But all these worketh that one and the selfsame Spirit, dividing to every man severally as he will." (I Corinthian 12:1-11)

" For as the body is one, and hath many members, and all the members of that one body, being many, are one body: so also is Christ.

¹³ For by one Spirit are we all baptized into one body, whether we be Jews or Gentiles, whether we be bond or free; and have been all made to drink into one Spirit." (I Corinthians 12:12)

It's again important to see that the gifts are listed in the context of a teaching related to the body of Christ. They are all given by the Holy Spirit and are for the purpose of edification and ministry…so that there would be no schism (division) in the body.

They were intended to bring the various believers together, (Jew & Gentile), as one, reliant upon each other to get the job done.

One believer cannot have all the gifts because the body is comprised of many members operating with several gifts each but not all gifts.

See what is taught about the body in the next paragraph.

> *"For the body is not one member, but many.* [15] *If the foot shall say, because I am not the hand, I am not of the body; is it therefore not of the body?* [16] *And if the ear shall say, because I am not the eye, I am not of the body; is it therefore not of the body?* [17] *If the whole body were an eye, where were the hearing? If the whole were hearing, where is the smelling?*
>
> [18] *But now hath God set the members every one of them in the body, as it hath pleased him.* [19] *And if they were all one member, where is the body?* [20] *But now are they many members, yet but one body.* [21] *And the eye cannot say unto the hand, I have no need of thee: nor again the head to the feet, I have no need of you.* [22] *Nay, much more those members of the body, which seem to be more feeble, are necessary:* [23] *And those members of the body, which we think to be less honorable, upon these we bestow more abundant honor; and our uncomely parts have more abundant comeliness.*
>
> [24] *For our comely parts have no need: but God hath tempered the body together, having given more abundant honor to that part which lacked.* [25] *That there should be no schism in the body; but that the members should have the same care one for another.*
>
> [26] *And whether one member suffer, all the members suffer with it; or one member be honored, all the members rejoice with it.* [27] *Now ye are the body of Christ, and members in particular."* (I Crointhians12: 14-27)

"*And God hath set some in the church, first apostles, secondarily prophets, thirdly teachers, after that miracles, then gifts of healings, helps, governments, diversities of tongues.* ^{29} *Are all apostles? are all prophets? Are all teachers?*

Are all workers of miracles? ^{30} *Have all the gifts of healing? Do all speak with tongues? Do all interpret?* ^{31} *But covet earnestly the best gifts: and yet shew I unto you a more excellent way."* (I Corinthians 12:28-31)

Which gifts are better? Isn't the best gift the one that meets the need? We need to discover the gifts that are already operating in us and utilize them for the ministry and glory of God. Holy Spirit gifts are not such things as being a good wife or mother or some other expected talent. They Are All Supernatural Gifts.

Here are some gifts and definitions that are evident in I Corinthians 12:28-31.

12:8 Word of Wisdom and Word of Knowledge…these are two gifts that are supernatural in nature. They operate by the Holy Spirit and are focused to specific events or problems that allow the believer to experience foreknowledge or to obtain the ability to utilize that knowledge that would otherwise not be known. These gifts usually operate together.

12:9 Faith …to be firmly persuaded of God's power and promises; to accomplish His will and purpose and to display such a confidence in Him and His Word that circumstances and obstacles do not shake that conviction.

12:9 Gifts of Healing... to be used as a means through which God makes people whole physically, emotionally, mentally, or spiritually. They are gifts of Healing, not just one.

12:10 The Working of Miracles... to be enabled by God to perform mighty deeds, which glorify God. They are of supernatural origin and means.

12:10 Prophecy...to speak forth the message of God to His people (Greek Word: prophets - the forth-telling of the will of God; 'pro'=forth; 'phemi'=to speak)

12:10 Discerning of Spirits...The ability to discern the Spirit of God, the spirit of the Flesh and the spirit of the devil in everyday life.

12:10 Diverse kinds of tongues and their interpretations...This gift of tongues is given to believers as a heavenly language so that they can communicate spirit to Spirit with God. The experience edifies the believer as his or her spirit speaks mysteries. Should this be part of a public gathering, it must be conducted in order and must be accompanied by an interpretation so all can be blessed.

Question? Are the gifts no longer needed in the body of Christ? At first glace, Paul's word to the Corinthians seem to agree with the idea of diminishing gifts.

> **I Corinthians 13:8-11** says, *"Charity, (Love), never fails: but whether there be prophecies, they shall fail; whether there be tongues, they shall cease; whether there be knowledge, it shall vanish away. ⁹ For we know in part, and we prophesy in part. ¹⁰ But when that which is perfect is come, then that which is in part shall be done away. ¹¹ When I was a child, I spake as a child, I understood as a child, I thought as a child: but when I became a man, I put away childish things."*

Take another look at verse 10, "But when that which is perfect is come, then that which is in part shall be done away"

We see in part. That's why we need the gifts. It is the Holy Spirit's way of uniting the body but it is still seeing in part, not fully. This is evident in the type of gift given. For example: A Word of Wisdom and A Word of Knowledge.

They are just a bit, not all but just a part. Tongues are the same because it requires an interpreter.

However, when that which is perfect is come, meaning Jesus at His 2nd coming, we will see in a full and complete view, leaving no more need for that which was in part, or gifts. Until that time, the gifts are needed to bring the body together for ministry here on earth. Sadly, the enemy has distorted the idea and confused the teaching causing a great divide.

The biggest issue is found in speaking in tongues. This has divided many a fellowship. Some use the gift to edify themselves and communicate spirit to Spirit with God. Others insist that this century has no need for tongues and they, with all the rest of the gifts, were stopped with the death of the apostles.

Here's some food for thought.

1. The gifts validated Jesus' claim that He was the Messiah, the Christ. They were bestowed upon His followers to continue that validation. Why would that not be needed now in our generation?

2. The gifts were given to the followers of Jesus to help the body to grow and become one. The words of wisdom, knowledge, miracles, and even tongues were all aimed at bringing unity and purpose to God's people. Isn't that still needed in today's world?

3. There are way more people in today's world than back in Jesus' day. Isn't the need for Holy Spirit power through the gifts needed more now that ever before?

4. The apostles laid hands on new believers, that were not apostles, and they received the gifts and began to operate in

them. They were passed on and on from anointed believer to new converts. Why would that need to stop?

Satan's deception is obvious in this matter. He has deceived many in believing they do not need even one Holy Spirit gift because it is a thing of the past.

This is a practical stripping of power and steeling of authority. If you do not believe that you can discern spirits, you'll never try.

If you do not believe that God can and will give you a word of wisdom or a word of knowledge, you'll miss out on His will and end up groping in the dark for answers. The gifts are more needed today than ever before and we really do need to seek God for the best gifts that suit our Christian walk.

WITH EAGLES' WINGS

I mounted up with Eagles' Wings
To soar above the clouds.
I viewed life above its trials,
Separate from the crowds.

Just me and God, together in the day,
His love to behold.
With Eagles' Wings, He led the way,
My future to unfold.

Forgiveness and peace in a distance,
Suddenly I could see.
Joy and happiness trailed behind
Then overshadowed me.

With Eagles' Wings,
I soar above life's every trial.
Now I walk by word of faith,
Rejoicing with every mile.

Written By
John Marinelli

CHAPTER TWENTY-THREE

The Body of Christ
Believe It or Not

The first epistle, (Letter), to the Corinthians was written by the apostle Paul to address some problems, which had arisen in the church at Corinth. In the early chapters of the epistle, Paul addressed the Corinthian believers concerning unity, fornication, discipline, and marriage.

The Corinthians also appear to have had some problems in the area of public worship, for Paul moved on to address the subjects of the Lord's Supper and the use of spiritual gifts within the local assembly.

The Body of Christ includes all "Born Again" believers, not all church members or all religions.

> "By one spirit are we all baptized into one body." (1 Cor.12:13)

Two factors are involved here.

1. First, there is a body, which is the Church. (Eph. 1:22,23)

2. Second, a person becomes a part of "The Body" by a baptism, not by water but by the Holy Spirit. BAPTISM:

means To Place Into, or On; For The Purpose of Identification.

"John baptized with water, but Jesus Christ will baptize with the Holy Spirit." (Mathew 3:11)

This was a reference to the Day of Pentecost which took place after the resurrection and ascension of Jesus Christ back into heaven - see Acts 1:5-8 and Acts 2:1-5.

From heaven, the Lord Jesus Christ "Poured Out" or placed His Spirit upon that believing remnant of Israel, just as John the Baptist promised and as was predicted in Joel 2:28-32.

This is also the baptism to which Paul refers in Ephesians 4:1-6.

"Endeavoring to keep the unity of the Spirit in the bond of peace. There is one body, and one Spirit, even as ye are called in one hope of your calling; One Lord, one faith, one baptism, One God and Father of all, who is above all, and through all, and in you all."

All is a reference to believers, not unbelievers.

Paul uses the human body as a metaphor to describe the Church. In Eph. 4:15,16, he said,

"Christ: from whom the whole body fitly joined together and compacted by that which every joint supplies, according to the effectual working in the measure of every part, makes increase of the body unto the edifying of itself in love."

Paul got this partly from Psalm 122:3.

"Jerusalem is built as a city that is compacted together."

Again, in Eph. 2:21,22, he said,

"In whom all the building fitly framed together grows

unto an holy temple in the Lord: In whom ye also are built together for an habitation of God through the Spirit."

Obviously these statements can in no way be used to describe Christianity in general. It is the destiny of all true believers.

Of all the cities in Israel, God chose Jerusalem to "put His name there." Even so, of all the groups in the Christian faith, God will yet choose one group from among all of the groups, which make up Christianity, to put His name there. (Mal. 3:16-18)

Later, in His prayer with His Twelve, He said to the Father,

"Keep through thine own name those whom Thou hast given me. While I was with them in the world, I kept them in Thy name." (John 17:11,12).

They were the spiritual city, which God had chosen to put His name. All the redeemed are noted in The Book of Life, but those in the Body of Christ are written in another book also.

This is made clear in Rev. 22:19.

"God shall take away his part out of The Book of Life, and out of the Holy City."

The same point is made in Heb. 12:22,23.

"Ye are come unto the city of the living God, the heavenly Jerusalem, the church of the firstborn which are written in heaven."

(Some paragraphs are excerpts from *Christ Series*, authored by C. Elden McNabb.)

He That Believes

"He that believes on me, as the scripture hath said, out of

his belly (innermost being) shall flow rivers of living water. (But this spake he of the Spirit, which they that believe on him should receive: for the Holy Ghost was not yet given; because that Jesus was not yet glorified.)" (John 7:38-39)

So, from the day of Pentecost, when the Holy Ghost was given… to our current day and until Jesus returns, believers are being added to the church, which is His body.

Once the Rapture occurs and at the Marriage Supper of the Lamb, we will become the Bride of Christ and as events unfold, end up dwelling with Christ on a new earth, fashioned just for us for all eternity. How great is that?

CHAPTER TWENTY-FOUR

Joint Heirs With Christ

Paul says, *"Now if we are children, then we are heirs—heirs of God and joint-heirs with Christ, if indeed we share in his sufferings in order that we may also share in his glory."* Romans 8:17

According to this verse, we share in the sufferings of Christ now and will share in the glory of Christ later as His "co-heirs" or "joint-heirs."

The term, *heirs of God*, emphasizes our relationship to God the Father. As His children, we have "an inheritance that can never perish, spoil or fade . . . kept in heaven" (1 Peter 1:4).

The Greek term translated "heirs" in Romans 8:17 refers to "those who receive their allotted possession by right of sonship." In other words, because God has made us His children (see John 1:12), we have full rights to receive His inheritance. We are His beneficiaries (see Matthew 25:34; Galatians 3:29; Colossians 1:12; 3:24).

Jesus, the only begotten Son of God, is the natural "heir" of the Father. "God said to him,

"You are my Son; today I have become your Father" (Hebrews 5:5; cf. Psalm 2:7).

Christ's inheritance is the whole universe all that is in existence.

Hebrews 1:2 says that the Son has been *"appointed heir of all things."* Being a joint-heir with Christ means that we, as God's adopted children, will share in the inheritance of Jesus. What belongs to Jesus will also belong to us. Christ gives us His glory (John 17:22), His riches (2 Corinthians 8:9), and all things (Hebrews 1:2).

We are as welcome in God's family as Jesus is; we are "accepted in the Beloved" (Ephesians 1:6). All that belongs to Jesus Christ will belong to us, the joint-heirs, as well.

"You are no longer a slave, but God's child; and since you are his child, God has made you also an heir" (Galatians 4:7). Think of what all that means.

Everything that God owns belongs to us as well because we belong to Him. Our eternal inheritance as joint-heirs with Christ is the result of the amazing grace of God.

Ephesians 2:13 says,

> *"In Christ Jesus you who once were far away have been brought near by the blood of Christ."*

God made us a part of His family through faith in Jesus Christ. He has showered us with blessings and promised us an eternal inheritance, based on the worthiness of Christ Himself.

Joint Heirs

Open To All Who Believe

This was not limited to just the Jews.

> *"That the gentiles should be fellow heirs, and of the same*

body, and partakers of his promise by Christ in the gospel".
Ephesians 3:6

There is, however, one qualifier to be a child of God and a Joint Heir with Jesus to the Kingdom of God.

Mainstream Christianity is moving more and more liberal. Many deny that Jesus is the only way to God. They openly declare that we are all children of God, some even say, children of the gods.

It was Jesus that said,

> *"For God so loved the world, that he gave his only begotten Son, that whosoever believeth in him should not perish, but have everlasting life."* John 3:16;

Jesus also saith unto him,

> *"I am the way, the truth, and the life: no man cometh unto the Father, but by me."* John 14:6;

Jesus answered and said unto him, (Nicodemus)

> *"Verily, verily, I say unto thee, except a man be born again, he cannot see the kingdom of God."* John 3:3

So, Sonship is dependent on being "Born Again" They that believe in Jesus as the only begotten Son of God are the same that receive eternal life and become the children of God and Joint Heirs with Christ.

How To Know You Are A Child of God

> *"The Spirit Himself bears witness with our spirit that we are children of God, and if children, then heirs—heirs of God and joint heirs with Christ."* Romans 8:15

The Spirit confirms your status with God. If you were really Born Again, God's Holy Spirit will communicate with you in little and big ways to let you know you are a child of God. I remember what happened to me years ago.

I opened the King James Bible and began to read the Psalms, the 4-Gospels and the Epistles. After a while, truth began to spring up as though it were jumping off the page into me heart.

These 'truth-bursts' were promises, directions, doctrines and guidance. Sometimes it was a blessing and other times it was a rebuke against my actions.

Many times it was a revelation that would shape my thinking and change my beliefs on certain topics or social issues.

It's been over 60 years now that the Holy Spirit has been talking to me through the Bible. He never stops. He is always there with comfort, guidance, love and respect.

Our Inheritance

"The Divine Nature"
Excerpts of Dawn Bible Study Association

Our inheritence is having the divine nature of God dwelling in us. This is the Glory of God that is now bestowed on Jesus and through the Born Again experience is shared with us.

Think about it…members of the fallen and dying race would be given an opportunity of being associated with Jesus, the Christ as rulers in his kingdom, and sharing his glory, as well as the glory of the Creator. It was another hidden truth in plain sight until it was brought to light by Jesus and the apostles.

Paul refers to it as the…

> *"mystery which hath been hid from ages and from*

generations, but now is made manifest to his saints: to whom God would make known what is the riches of the glory of this mystery among the Gentiles; which is Christ in you, the hope of glory."—Col. 1:26,27

Paul wrote to Christians in Rome,

"By whom Christ we have access by faith into his grace wherein we stand, and rejoice in hope of the glory of God." (Rom. 5:2)

The meaning of the expression, *'glory of God'*, is quite beyond the ability of our finite minds to comprehend. However, various promises of the Bible give us an inkling of what it implies. As we have seen, when Jesus was raised from the dead, he was highly exalted to the divine nature, and to the right hand of God.

The apostle John wrote,

"Beloved, now are we the sons of God, and it doth not yet appear what we shall be: but we know that, when he shall appear, we shall be like him; for we shall see him as he is." (I John 3:2)

John realized the limitations of the human mind in understanding matters pertaining to the spirit world.

"It doth not yet appear what we shall be," he concedes, *"but we know that, ... we shall be like him* Christ

Yes, like Christ, to whom was given "all power in heaven and in earth"; like Christ who was made a "quickening spirit" that he might give life to the dead world of mankind; and like Christ who is now the "express image" of his Father's person, having partaken of his glory. (Matt. 28:18; I Cor. 15:45; Heb. 1:3)

These are some of the aspects of the *'glory of God'* to which the children of God are heirs. They have to do with the personal glory of God, the glory of the 'divine nature'.

> Peter writes that unto us have been given *"exceeding great and precious promises" that by these we might become "partakers of the divine nature."*—II Pet. 1:4

As Jesus was exalted to share his Father's throne, so we are promised, if faithful, that we shall sit with Jesus in his throne. (Rev. 3:21) Jesus is now the great King—the "King of kings," and his joint-heirs are to be made kings, to "reign with Jesus on the earth." (Rev. 5:10)

Our Inheritance

"The Power of God"

Another inheritance that is ours as a joint heir with Christ is "The Power of God."

> *"As many as received him, to them gave he power to become the sons of God, even to them that believe on his name: which were born, not of blood, nor of the will of the flesh, nor of the will of man, but of God."* John 1:12

> "Jesus said, *Verily, verily, I say unto you, He that believeth on me, the works that I do shall he do also; and greater works than these shall he do; because I go unto my Father. And whatsoever ye shall ask in my name, that will I do, that the Father may be glorified in the Son."* John 14:12-13

Paul picks up on this power as he writes to the Philippian church. He says,

> *"I can do "All Things" through Christ which strengthens me."* Philippians 4:13

He said he could and so can we, do "All Things" because as God gave Paul strength which is divine power, so shall He give us strength (Divine Power) to do, "All Things".

Thus the joint heir inheritance of Divine Power, like the Divine Nature, is available to us in this lifetime. We do not have to wait until we die and go to heaven. It is ours to appropriate now and use now to accomplish "All Things."

More of Our Inheritance As A Joint Heir With Jesus Christ

Taken From Got\Questions.com

The Bible is full of references to the inheritance believers have in Christ. Ephesians 1:11 says,

> *"In Christ we have obtained an inheritance, having been predestined according to the purpose of him who works all things according to the counsel of his will"* (ESV).

Other passages that mention a believer's inheritance include Colossians 3:24 and Hebrews 9:15.

Our inheritance is, in a word, Heaven. It is the sum total of all God has promised us in salvation. Words related to *inheritance* in Scripture are *portion* and *heritage*.

First Peter 1:4 describe this inheritance further, saying that we have been born again "into an inheritance that can never perish, spoil or fade. This inheritance is kept in heaven for you." According to the apostle Peter, our inheritance is distinguished by four important qualities:

Our Inheritance In Christ Is Imperishable. What we have in Christ is not subject to corruption or decay. In contrast, everything on earth is in the process of decaying, rusting, or falling apart.

The law of entropy affects our houses, our cars, and even our own bodies. Our treasure in heaven, though, is unaffected by entropy (Matthew 6:19–20). Those who have been born again are born…

> *"not of perishable seed, but of imperishable, through the living and enduring word of God"* (1 Peter 1:23).

Our Inheritance In Christ Is Unspoiled. What we have in Christ is free from anything that would deform, debase, or degrade. Nothing on earth is perfect. Even the most beautiful things of this world are flawed; if we look closely enough, we can always find an imperfection.

But Christ is truly perfect. He is "holy, blameless, pure, set apart from sinners, exalted above the heavens" (Hebrews 7:26), and our inheritance in Him is also holy, blameless, exalted, and pure. No earthly corruption or weakness can touch what God has bestowed. Revelation 21:27 says

> *"nothing impure will ever enter [the New Jerusalem], nor will anyone who does what is shameful or deceitful."*

Our Inheritance In Christ Is Unfading. What we have in Christ is an enduring possession. As creatures of this world, it is hard for us to imagine colors of that never fade, excitement that never flags, or value that never depreciates; but our inheritance is not of this world. Its glorious intensity will never diminish.

> God says, *"I am making everything new!"* (Revelation 21:5).

Our Inheritance In Christ Is Reserved. What we have in Christ is being "kept" in heaven for us. Your crown of glory has your name on it.

Although we enjoy many blessings as children of God here on

earth, our true inheritance—our true home—is reserved for us in heaven. Like Abraham, we are…

> *"looking forward to the city with foundations, whose architect and builder is God"* (Hebrews 11:10).

The Holy Spirit guarantees that we will receive eternal life in the world to come (2 Corinthians 1:22).

> In fact, *"when you believed, you were marked in him with a seal, the promised Holy Spirit, who is a deposit guaranteeing our inheritance"* (Ephesians 1:13–14).

Jesus prayed for His followers,

> *"Holy Father, protect them by the power of your name"* (John 17:11).

We are secure, being guarded by the Almighty Himself, and surely our inheritance is equally secure. No one can steal it from us. John 10:28–29:

> *"I give them eternal life, and they shall never perish; no one will snatch them out of my hand. My Father, who has given them to me, is greater than all; no one can snatch them out of my Father's hand."* See also Matthew 6:20.

As God's children, "adopted" into His family, we have been assured an inheritance from our Heavenly Father.

> *"Now if we are children, then we are heirs—heirs of God and co-heirs with Christ, if indeed we share in his sufferings in order that we may also share in his glory"* (Romans 8:17).

This heavenly heritage is God's purpose and will for us (Ephesians

1:11). We receive the promise of our inheritance by hearing the word of truth and believing in Christ (Ephesians 1:13).

One day, we will take possession of our portion, our heritage, and our full inheritance. John Calvin writes of our inheritance, "We do not have the full enjoyment of it at present. We walk in hope, and we do not see the thing as if it were present, but we see it by faith."

Seeing that the Holy Spirit reigns in our hearts, we have something for which to give praise even in the midst of all our temptations. Therefore, we should rejoice, mourn, grieve, give thanks, be content, wait" (from Calvin's Ephesian sermons, delivered in Geneva, 1558—59).

When we understand and value the glory that awaits us, we are better able to endure whatever comes our way in this life. We can give God praise even during trials because we have His guarantee that we will receive all He has promised:

> *"For our light and momentary troubles are achieving for us an eternal glory that far outweighs them all"* (2 Corinthians 4:17).

Revelation 21:4 gives us a brief but beautiful description of our inheritance: "'He will wipe every tear from their eyes. There will be no more death' or mourning or crying or pain, for the old order of things has passed away." God and man will dwell together. Everything will be made new.

The New Jerusalem, will be our residence. The river of life will issue from God's throne. The healing tree of life with twelve kinds of fruit will grow there, too. There will be no night there, because the eternal light of the Lamb will fill the new heaven and new earth and shine upon all the heirs of God.

King David writes,

> *"Lord, you alone are my portion and my cup; you make*

my lot secure. The boundary lines have fallen for me in pleasant places; surely I have a delightful inheritance" (Psalm 16:5–6).

And that is why "we fix our eyes not on what is seen, but on what is unseen, since what is seen is temporary, but what is unseen is eternal" (2 Corinthians 4:18).

We have to be like Abraham and not waver at the promises God has for us. Romans 4:20-21

"He did not waver at the promise of God through unbelief, but was strengthened in faith, giving glory to God, and being fully convinced that what He had promised He was also able to perform."

Heirs of What?

Excerpts From The Bible Hub

The children of God are heirs of God's Promises. If you turn to the 1st chapter of the Epistle to the Hebrews, the 14th verse, you will find that we are there called *"heirs of salvation."* Looking on a little further in the same Epistle, in the 6th chapter, and the 17th verse, you will find that we are called "the heirs of promise."

In his Epistle to Titus, the 3rd chapter, and the 7th verse, Paul calls us *"heirs according to the hope of eternal life"*; while James says, in the 2nd chapter of his Epistle, at the 5th verse, that we are *"heirs of the kingdom which God hath promised to them that love him"*; and Peter says, in his First Epistle, the 3rd chapter, and 7th verse, that we are *"heirs together of the grace of life."*

We are heirs of God's Possessions. When God gives Himself to us, He gives us with Himself all that He has. And this means treasures vast and immeasurable.

The stars in their glittering splendor are the dust of His feet. The kingdoms of the world are to Him the small dust of the balance. Writing to the Corinthians, Paul says: "All things are yours; whether Paul, or Apollos, or Cephas, or the world, or life, or death, or things present, or things to come; all are yours."

We are heirs of God's Attributes. Is He omnipotent? His omnipotence is ours, to be our defense. Is He omniscient? His infinite wisdom is ours, to guide us. Is He eternal? His eternity is ours, that we may ever be preserved. Is He full of love and grace?

Then all His love, as though there were not another to be loved, is mine, and all His grace, as though there were never another sinner to partake of it, is mine. "The Lord is the portion of mine inheritance and of my cup." "God is the strength of my heart, and my portion for ever."

> *"For whom he did foreknow, he also did predestinate to be conformed to the image of his Son, that he (The Son) might be the firstborn among many brethren."*

He cannot possibly be heir alone; for union with Christ is the very reason why we are heirs of God, and union with Christ must for us also culminate in glory. The inheritance is sure because Christ possesses it now.

Our right to sonship and being a child of God stands or falls with Christ's right to the same inheritance. We are Joint-Heirs; if He be truly an heir, so are we; and if He be not, neither are we. Our two interests are intertwined and made one, we have neither of us any heirship apart from the other; we are joint-heirs, Christ jointly with us, ourselves jointly with Christ.

So, then, it follows that if there be any flaw in the will, so that it be not valid, if it be not rightly signed, sealed, and delivered, then it is no more valid for Christ than it is for us.

If we get nothing, Christ gets nothing; if there should be no heaven for us, there is no heaven for Christ. If there should be no throne for us, there would be no throne for Him; if the promise should utterly fail of fulfillment to the least of the joint-heritors, it must also fail of accomplishment to our Lord Jesus Christ Himself. [Note: C. H. Spurgeon.]

And this lets us see how great the inheritance is. If we are to be joint-heirs with Christ, it cannot be a little thing that we are to share with Him.

Can you imagine what the Father would give to His Son as the reward of the travail of His soul? Give yourself time to think what the everlasting God would give to His equal Son, "who took upon Himself the form of a servant, and was made in the likeness of men, and who humbled Himself, and became obedient unto death, even the death of the cross." Philippians 2:7 Can you think of a reward that would be large enough for Him? Let the Father's love and the Father's justice judge.

Jesus said,

> *"All things have been delivered to me by my Father; and no one knows the Son except the Father, and no one knows the Father except the Son and any one to whom the Son chooses to reveal him."* Matthew 11:27

We are they to whom the Son chooses to reveal Himself. We are those that have been destined to conformity as the Joint Heir of Christ. The whole purpose of such an event is so Jesus would be the "First Born" among many brethren.

Our future is assured, actually pre-determined. We have a Heavenly calling that includes a destiny that is almost beyond belief. We are to be like Christ. We are to be the inheritors of the Kingdom of God.

We suffer now in this life, here on this earth, as we face many hardships and trials. However, our suffering is but a light affliction when compared to what has been stored up for us in Glory. We will reign with Him over all that there is, was and will ever be. How great is that?

Knowing now what will soon come, what manor of man or woman ought we to be? Would it be safe to say, "We ought to allow Jesus to reign in our hearts as Lord so He can lead us down the path of righteousness into the full inheritance that is ours"?

Remember, not every Christian will realize the status of "Sonship" The children of God are those who have been "Born Again" by the spirit of God. We cannot attain a joint-Heir status by joining a church or following a Dos and Don't list. We must repent, receive Jesus as Lord and Savor. This is how we get born again and become a child of God. This is the path to being a Joint-Heir with Christ.

CONCLUSION

We have looked at many Bible truths that were hidden in plain sight. I hope you have been blessed, edified and able to walk away with a greater appreciation for the Word of God

I have only touched on the surface of these Biblical truths. I tried to utilize other scholars and students of the Bible so you wouldn't conclude that the opinions expressed in this book were exclusively mine. I hope you were challenged to, *"Think About It."* You can, "Believe It or Not."

It is high time for Christians to be believers and walk in the teaching of Jesus. This is the true way to walk in the Spirit and not the flesh. I realize also that some, if not most of my readers, are seeking the Lord and are o.k. with their Christian walk.

If in fact that is you, I hope you have been refreshed in the Word and encouraged to continue in your faith.

If this book has been a blessing to you, please email me and let me know.

johnmarinelli@embarqmail.com.

"No Weapon formed against you will prosper."

Isaiah 54:17

BETWEEN HEAVEN AND YOU

I am sorry you're down today;
It is not easy to walk My way.
There are trials on every side,
Even darkness where Satan hides.

But that's no reason to be blue;
Your Heavenly Father still loves you.
He sees the burden you now bear;
I have made Him keenly aware.

I stand between heaven and you
To insure you make it through.
I will send My love your way,
So be at peace – watch and pray!

God is on your every side;
He alone will turn the tide.
And what now makes you blue,
Will suddenly depart from you.

Written By
John Marinelli

ABOUT THE AUTHOR

Rev. John Marinelli

Rev. Marinelli is an ordained minister, He has formed and been pastor of one church in Wisconsin and was the pastor of another in Alabama. He has also been a youth minister and evangelism director over the years.

Rev. Marinelli has authored several books including: "Original Story Poems", "The Art of Writing Christian Poetry," "Pulpit Poems," "Moonlight & Mistletoe," "The Mysterious Stranger," "With Eagles Wings," "Mysteries & Miracles," "It Came To Pass," Why Do The Righteous Suffer," and "Believer's Handbook of Battle Strategies."

John is an accomplished Christian poet. He also dabbles in songwriting and writing one act Christian plays.

He is the Vice President of Have A Heart For Companion Animals, Inc., a "No Kill" animal welfare organization...

www.haveaheart.us

Rev. Marinelli is now retired from the sales and marketing arena after spending over 40 years in business-to-business and non-profit marketing.

Rev. Marinelli enjoys writing Christian fiction stories, playing chess, singing karaoke and a retired lifestyle in sunny Florida.

For More Info or eMail Communication
Contact johnmarinelli@embarqmail.com

The End

www.ingramcontent.com/pod-product-compliance
Lightning Source LLC
Chambersburg PA
CBHW020419010526
44118CB00010B/330